MANAGING PEOPLE IN A DOWNTURN

MANAGING PEOPLE IN A DOWNTURN

Adrian Furnham

Professor of Psychology
University College London, UK

First published 2011 by
PALGRAVE MACMILLAN

Palgrave Macmillan in the UK is an imprint of Macmillan Publishers Limited, registered in England, company number 785998, of Houndmills, Basingstoke, Hampshire RG21 6XS.

Palgrave Macmillan in the US is a division of St Martin's Press LLC, 175 Fifth Avenue, New York, NY 10010.

Palgrave Macmillan is the global academic imprint of the above companies and has companies and representatives throughout the world.

Palgrave® and Macmillan® are registered trademarks in the United States, the United Kingdom, Europe and other countries.

ISBN 978–0–230–29854–5

This book is printed on paper suitable for recycling and made from fully managed and sustained forest sources. Logging, pulping and manufacturing processes are expected to conform to the environmental regulations of the country of origin.

A catalogue record for this book is available from the British Library.

A catalog record for this book is available from the Library of Congress.

10 9 8 7 6 5 4 3 2 1
20 19 18 17 16 15 14 13 12 11

Printed and bound in Great Britain by
MPG Group, Bodmin and King's Lynn

For Alison and Benedict... always

Contents

Preface

Last year, I delivered lectures and training sessions in 22 countries. I did this at universities, but also for organizations like airlines, banks and pharmaceutical companies. It was a bad year for business. In London and Dubai, the many cranes weren't moving. Everything seemed to be "on hold" until the good times returned again. Its tough out there; particularly for managers.

I am, however, impressed by how homogeneous the world is becoming. Education and the Internet are reducing cultural issues, along with worldwide trade and migration. Yet, there remain subtle but important national, ethnic and corporate culture issues that can bewilder and frustrate any manager with a culturally diverse workforce.

Three things, however, strike me about the world of business. The *first* is that management problems are much *the same the world over*. They always have been, and they always will be. Certainly, culture plays a part, as do where we are in the economic cycle but, overall, people-problems remain still the most vexing and the most common of all organizational problems. People are complex, capricious and cunning. Many love their jobs; and many do not! Many give their all; others seem alienated and disengaged. Some managers seem to get the most out their staff, even in the bad times; others struggle to do a good job, even in the good times.

Second, at least in the west, the major people-problem is presented as a *motivational* one. How do you motivate people from generation Y or the millennial? How do you teach managers to engage their staff? What things do you have to do in turbulent times? Is this different or simply better management? Why, paradoxically, is money such an expensive and ineffective motivator?

Whilst motivation and other people-problems are subtle, multi-faceted and complex, often the solutions presented are far from simple. There is clearly a demand–supply curve for magic bullet cures. Hence the market for gurus, business books and motivational consultants. Why are there so many simple answers to a complex problem? An analogy could be diet books and the diet industry. Diets, they say, are bad for you because, paradoxically, they lead to weight gain. One really needs a life-style change – which is neither easy nor simple, but works. Developing, motivating and directing a team, which is the heart of business leadership, has never been easy. But there are straightforward principles to follow and skills to acquire.

Third, the next most commonly defined problem is *change*. Note that the word change is used as opposed to *progress*. Managers worry about changing customer expectations, changing workforce motivation and diversity, as well as changes to organizational structure. Change hurts, and hence the quest for an efficient way of doing it well and, if possible, painlessly. And change is often not an option: it is a necessity.

Of course, the problems of management are made much worse during down-turns: in bear rather than bull markets.

This book covers these topics, and more besides. It is a collection of 74 essays, diatribes and thought-pieces. Some are deliberately iconoclastic; others just a little naughty. Some have appeared in my newspaper columns, others in specialized magazines. They have been written in airline lounges and on villa verandas. I have noted down odd phrases and curious events in commercial settings, and tried to make sense of them by scribbling. The aim is to provide three things. *First*, a skeptical sideways look at some business issues that maybe too politically incorrect or career-limiting for people in organizations to say. That is, of course, if they agree with me.

The *second* aim is to discuss some recent academic papers in a jargon-free and approachable way. Academic papers are not often read by managers or gurus. Whilst some are written in impenetrable prose with complex statistics, they often have very interesting ideas and findings that merit reaching the light of day. Some of the essays attempt to do just this.

Third, I hope to amuse. What goes on in "the office" is so often so patently absurd, bizarre and ridiculous it becomes good material for sit-coms. Indeed, one called *The Office* was a huge success. As they say, "you have to laugh" at the things that go on at work in the name of management. It's a fine coping strategy, and an excellent way to puncture the superciliousness and pomposity of senior managers and consultants.

As ever, I have a few people to thank for inspiring my ideas. They include Robert Hogan, John Taylor and David Pendelton. But, most of all, my clever and elegant wife through whose hands these scribblings have to pass before they reach publication. I have a great deal of "Re-write by Tuesday" and "Report to my study immediately." My efforts are always better for the intervention of my no-nonsense editrix. But I strive always to do better, I hope it shows!

ADRIAN FURNHAM

Introduction

The most frequently asked management question from nearly all supervisors and managers (and teachers and trainers) to CEOs, certainly in developed Western countries, is **how to increase the work motivation** of their staff. What they all want is to have employees with the work ethic: conscientious, dedicated, dependable, dutiful, reliable, responsible and responsive. They want them to be good at, and enjoy, their jobs like they (supposedly) do and, it has to be admitted, not to have to pay them "top dollar" for the privilege – in short, to be strongly intrinsically motivated.

There used to be that simple old distinction called Theory X and Theory Y. Theory X said: Most people dislike work and try to avoid it; most have no ambition and want no authority; most are self-centered and resist change; most are dim and gullible. They only work for money and security. So be tough and ruthless. Try the old command and control approach: keep them cold and keep them hungry, and they might be motivated to try harder.

Theory Y argues that work can be as satisfying as rest and play. People can be committed, happy and productive at work. If their "higher needs" of self-fulfillment are met they can become engaged, creative and responsible. If you follow this model, the recommended style of management is participative and stresses decentralization and delegation.

Most believe that through careful selection, good training and skilled management, it is possible to have a happy, healthy and highly productive work-force – or is it? So what is the secret? Whence the magic bullet? Indeed, is it naïve to believe there is one?

Paradoxically, there is very little new in motivation research. What we know to be important and efficacious, we have known for many years. That, of course, does not mean that people read it or follow the advice of researchers or wise managers. Whether you ask people what motivates them, or do careful case studies or organizations with especially high or low levels of organization, or even talk to consultants, the story is much the same. They are intrinsically motivated and well-managed; equitably rewarded and well-adjusted people.

Interestingly, you can derive lists of things that de-motivate people as easily as you can lists that motivate people. And, as one may expect, the lists mirror one another. That is, if a certain feature at work is non-existent or of poor quality and/or quantity, and is rated important, the result is serious de-motivation. There are sins of omission as well as commission in the business of motivation.

First, there are various factors that influence motivation. Around a dozen are frequently listed. But it is only a relatively small number that have a powerful impact. The most motivated of individuals can be thwarted, frustrated and de-motivated by incompetent managers. *Second*, managers often place too much emphasis on less important, sometimes trivial, factors – missing out those they choose not to confront. In this sense, there remain many myths of management. *Third*, it is true that there are some differences in motivational issues, depending on the business; and there may be corporate and national culture differences, and even some affects of the sector and size of the organization.

But the biggest factor is usually associated with the workforce. There is evidence that the employer's age, gender, education and management level does have a profound effect on what motivates them, and how that process works. Women place a somewhat different emphasis on certain factors than do men. Also, quite naturally, the 25-year-old and 55-year-old have rather different concerns and priorities for what they really want at work. Equally, management grade or level makes some difference, though this is related to other factors like age, education and length of service. Senior staff have different expectations and experiences than junior staff.

One size does not fit all. Hardly rocket science – but an important fact frequently reflected in the different balance of "packages contents" of "comp. and ben." for different types of jobs.

But it is important not to overemphasize the differences. These are of magnitude, not kind. There are universals. So what are they?

First, working relationships. We are social animals. We spend eight or so hours a day at work. We interact with colleagues who often become close friends. We have relationships **up** (with a boss), **across** (with peers, colleagues), **down** (those who report to us) and **out** (with customers, shareholders and the like). They are different types of relationships – but all are important.

Ensure that the work-group is open, supportive and trusting of each other and of management, and you are half-way there. It is not that easy a task, and one that requires regular maintenance. People at work, are, at once, both a source of pleasure and pain, heaven and hell – as are other people. Relationships at work can both cause and "bust" stress. They can lead people to go the extra mile or fall at the first hurdle.

This is why we hear such a lot about team work and team building. We don't have to bond together, but we do have to pull together. Be part of a successful team that offers support, friendship and help, and most people care less about extrinsic factors like pay and conditions. All people at work need emotional, informational, technical and financial support. But this does not happen by accident. And it does not occur after a weekend of outdoor pursuits or seminars at a nice country hotel.

Second, and related to this, is the fact that it is one's direct boss that can make the greatest difference. What do people want in their boss? Perception, fairness and helpfulness; honesty, competence and inspiration; and, of particular importance, integrity. People usually don't resign from organizations: they leave individual bosses. The military have known this for years. Offices make all the difference. Management style and values, and competencies and skills, are one of the best predictors of staff motivation. A manager's skill, personality and values are crucial predictors of worker motivation. Hence the recent idea of the leadership profit chain. The idea is simply this: most people are in business to make money. That is best achieved by happy, enthusiastic repeat customers. And is achieved by attentive, loyal and trained staff, which is the supervisor's primary responsibility. They, in turn, report to managers/leaders who not only set direction, but also motivate the supervisors. Hence the chain from leadership to profit.

Third, people need to be helped to read, and be recognized for reaching their potential. Call it "positive feedback" or "positive strokes." Call it "recognition" or "reinforcement," call it "praise" or "thanks." It is absolutely fundamental. And it's cheap. And we often don't do it enough. There are dozens of ways of recognizing people for their effort and dedication. Further, this has the desirable effect of increasing it. All parents, teachers and trainers know this. Odd that many managers do not.

Fourth, people like interesting, varied, absorbing work. Not all jobs can provide this, but they can all be enriched. Many like to solve problems. All want the feeling that they have some control; that they have some say in how and where they do their job. The physical environment can play a part, but don't assume that it can compensate for any of the above factors. The idea is to make the job intrinsically interesting: that is, interesting for its own sake.

Fifth – and note it is fifth, and not first – they want their salary and package to reflect their comparative skill, dedication and work. At various life stages, other things like job security or time off work appear to be more valuable than money, but never underestimate the usefulness of the symbolism of money. Remember the issue of managing volunteers who are not paid. How to motivate them: the answer must be especially good management. Of course, they are different from conscripts in their values and outlook. But like anyone else, they want to be thoughtfully managed.

And, oh yes! You can't compensate with nice offices and fancy job titles. It is not difficult and it's not rocket science. Foster good working relationships, train managers in people and technical skills; always recognize and reward good work; try to make the job intrinsically satisfying and pay people what they are worth. Set people stretching goals they can achieve. Help them on that journey. Give them feedback on how they are doing. It'll be worth it.

Approaches and theories to motivation

Business Management textbooks have long chapters on work motivation: they nearly all list different theories. They usually try to distinguish between conscious and unconscious motivation, intrinsic and extrinsic motivation, intra- and inter-personal factors. There are old theories and new theories: old wine in new skins and new skins around old wine. They certainly make good reading. They each seem to have part of the truth – but only part. They seem to overemphasize one facet of the whole process. But they can and do make interesting distinctions and are worth having a look at, albeit briefly and critically. I will consider just three aspects.

Intrinsic and extrinsic motivation

Why is a pilot paid more than a professor? Or a newsreader paid more than a nurse? There are many glib answers to this seemingly simple question. Market forces of supply and demand, selection and years of training, a history of trade union bargaining?

But one factor, recognized by everybody, is that intrinsically motivating jobs require less compensation than intrinsically less-motivating jobs. So, what then is the difference between intrinsic and extrinsic motivation? It can be illustrated by the following true story:

> An academic was working at home. Things were going well, but it was a holiday and the local park nearby was full of children laughing and playing. Their erratic, loud, uncontrollable noise was deeply disturbing. There was no easy alternative for the writer. Closing the windows did little to muffle the sound, only make

the room stuffy. There was no other room to decamp to. So what to do, other than ask the children to move on.

A number of possibilities arose: threaten the children or bribe them to go away. The children might accept the bribe but soon return to this lucrative source of cash. The academic however, knew his motivation theory. He wandered outside. Mustering all the charm he could, he gathered the children around him and told them that he had observed them from his office and had admired and enjoyed their noisy games, high-spirited yells and laughter-so much so that he was prepared to pay them to continue. Each child was given £1.50.

Of course, they continued. The wise old don did the same the next day and the next. It cost him nearly £20. But on the fourth day, when the expectant children gathered around, he explained that for various reasons he had no money so he could no longer continue to "subsidize" their play. Speaking on behalf of the others, the oldest child said that if he thought the children were going to carry on playing for nothing he was sadly misinformed, and they left. Never to return. Mission accomplished.

What the writer knew was that the essence of play is that it is intrinsically satisfying. It is a preposterous idea to pay people to play, because they love and volunteer for the activity. You only have to recompense people for doing things they do not really enjoy: things that are dangerous or mind-numbingly dreary; things that are tiring or stressful. Yet, by paying for the play, the academic persuaded the children to view it in a different way. They thought they were playing for money. Then stop the money and they stop playing.

In 1990, a psychologist called Csikszentmhyalyi wrote a book called *Flow*, which tried to describe and explain that magical state of pleasure that people get from doing a favorite activity. This may be hiking or hang-gliding, singing the Messiah in a full choir, or carefully tending a garden. These pastimes are, for enthusiasts, deeply satisfying experiences: engrossing and enriching, beguiling and rewarding. Yet, they are also very personal and appeal very differently to different people. In the world of work, some jobs offer many flow opportunities and some offer practically none at all.

Some jobs are simply rotten jobs. Traffic wardens, for example, are deeply loathed, frequently assaulted, out in all weathers, doing something no one respects them for. Or a ubiquitous security guard job: unbelievably tedious, occasionally dangerous; or working on a dreary production line in a noisy, dirty factory. Not easy to make those jobs intrinsically satisfying.

Two indicators of pay level are how long it takes to master the skill and knowledge to do the job, and the responsibilities that go with it. For example, training as an airline pilot takes years, and the responsibilities that go with the job are considerable. Every day, the pilot is responsible for many hundreds of human lives. By contrast, most academic professors do not have that sort of responsibility, although their training is usually much longer.

But how intrinsically motivating is it flying a jumbo jet? The answer is, not a great deal. Sophisticated automation means that, once airborne, much of the job is to monitor the dials. It is repetitive and the hours are long. Airline pilots' pay is high – much higher than professors who, in the UK at least, have seen their comparative incomes decline for most of the last century. Yet, there is still fierce competition for academic jobs. Why? The answer is: intrinsic motivation.

Whilst professors have both administrative and teaching responsibilities, they know that it is their research that leads to promotion. And what, where and why they research is left up to them. They may follow their passions and whims; exploit their talents as they feel fit. Labs and libraries are occupied at weekends, not out of extrinsic but, rather, intrinsic motivation. Professors often double their required hours of work, but do not get paid overtime. Indeed, the idea is preposterous. It is like paying children to play.

Naturally, there comes a point in all deeply intrinsically motivating jobs where people make the choice between lifestyles. People in the City of London are conspicuously extrinsically motivated. Many want high earnings so that they can retire at 40 or 50. They are prepared to put up with very long hours of stressful work for lots of money if it allows them to do something intrinsically motivating afterwards.

The motivational lessons are very clear: the more intrinsically motivating the job, the less extrinsic rewards are necessary, and vice versa. The trick, therefore, is to try and turn jobs into those that are intrinsically motivating. But there is a deeper lesson. Rewarding someone extrinsically (i.e. money) for something they like doing actually de-motivates them.

Pay people what they are worth in the market place. Don't make salaries public. Don't make a big thing about monetary reward. Help them find their strengths and exploit them. Treat them fairly; remember that they are social animals.

Unconscious and conscious motivation: The clinical perspective

Clinicians, of various persuasions, are very interested in motivators, though rarely specifically in the workplace. They are often asked to explain the bizarre, often self-defeating behavior of what most of us think as "mad men." There certainly is plenty of "pathology" in the office. Certain personality disorders often seem a "course requirement" – or, at least, an asset – at work: narcissistic personality disorder or anti-social personality disorder. The obsessive compulsive may be valued in the quality control or health and safety departments, whilst a "touch of paranoia" certainly seems to do little harm in the security department.

People with an astonishing array of disorders still seem to thrive at work. There are bi-polars and phobics; psychopaths and depressives; hysterics and near autistics who hold down and thrive in good jobs.

The business world has a view of organizational man as a rational, pleasure-maximizing, logical, homo-economicus. Clinicians, on the other hand, report anxieties, defenses, fantasies and self-destructive behavior. They see the workings of the un- and pre-conscious; long-forgotten and repressed memories and – more importantly – powerful motivational drives that seem deeply buried in the executive unconscious. People seem to follow scripts: they are in their own play: what Kets de Vries (2006) calls the "inner theatre."

The psychoanalysts (Freudian, Jungian and Kleinian) make certain assumptions – hold, as true, various axioms – that inform how they see all behavior, including that at work. *First*, all behavior is explicable. Even apparently illogical, irrational, destructive behavior has a "rational" explanation. With enough clever detective work, one can explain human behavior in terms of a limited number of powerful concepts.

Second, much of what motivates us is unconscious. One cannot easily or accurately know what motivates us, when or how. The reasons for thought, feelings and actions are below the surface. We don't have sufficient insight; we have too many blind spots, or even good motives, for being unable to say openly why we want things or behaving as we do. Indeed, that is the primary aim of therapy: to bring the un- and pre-conscious into consciousness. In this sense, people cannot – rather than will not – tell you what "really" motivates them.

Third, we are as much driven by the heart as by the head. Our day-to-day behavior, both in the workplace and out of it, is as much dictated by our emotional selves as our rational selves. The great enthusiasts for the concept of emotional intelligence bear witness to people recognizing the obvious fact. Most of our relationships are powerfully governed by our feelings.

Fourth, we are products, rather than captives or victims, of our past. Early life experiences of loss, of security, of trauma are carried into adulthood: hence all the speculation about being able to spot future CEOs in the playground. When they feel secure to do so, some senior business executives "look back," and report surprising and powerful experiences that have shaped them. Reports often refer to the ambitious mother, the inspirational teacher, the early social groups. This is where motivation is grounded and where it starts from.

Granted, clinicians are more likely to see the burnt-out and distressed manager, supervisor or teacher than those who seem to cope well. However, many have speculated about, and commented on, the often strange behavior of prominent leaders. Some have gone on to correctly predict their downfall.

One of the most important insights from this work is that many people "cannot," as opposed to "will not," tell others what really motivates them. Or worse, what they think motivates them is not really what motivates them. Greed, envy and covetousness are common motivators, though rarely talked about. What people say motivates them and what really motivates them are often very different things.

It takes time, insight and emotional intelligence to understand other people. We have to get along with and get ahead of people at the same time. We bring to work our hopes, anxieties and vulnerability. We spend one third of every day at work, often more. It is central to our lives. And it is the focus of so much of what we do. No wonder work motivation is so important but complex.

Values and vocational guidance approach

The "motto" of vocational guidance is to fit round pegs into round holes. It is to help somebody find a job that is compatible with their abilities, values and preferences. This nearly always involves researchers trying to categorize jobs and then to find categories of people that fit them.

An alternative approach is to ask people what sorts of things are important to them at work. Consider this fairly lengthy list:

1. **Balance** – a job that allows me to lead a balanced life.
2. **Benefits** – a job that provides many features additional to pay (e.g. pension top-ups, extra holidays).
3. **Bonuses** – a job that provides many opportunities for topping up the basic salary.
4. **Clarity** – a job with clear and well-defined roles and responsibilities.

5. **Comfort** – a job that can be carried out in physically comfortable conditions.
6. **Competition** – a job that provides me with opportunities to compete with others.
7. **Conditions** – a job that can be carried out in conditions that are safe, modern and clean.
8. **Contribution to society** – a job that allows me to work for a good cause.
9. **Effortlessness** – a job that is relatively easy and does not require excessive effort.
10. **Equipment** – a job that can be carried out with up-to-date equipment and technology.
11. **Flexibility** – a job that allows me to work flexible hours to suit my personal needs.
12. **Independence** – a job that allows me to work autonomously without much supervision.
13. **Insurance** – a job that provides health and life insurance.
14. **Intellectuality** – a job that is challenging and involves a great deal of thinking and analysis.
15. **Location** – a job that is conveniently located and accessible.
16. **Organizational image** – a job within an organization that is widely recognized and respected.
17. **Pay** – a job that is very well paid.
18. **Perks** – a job that provides many extras (e.g. company car, discounts on goods, and so on).
19. **Personal growth** – a job that provides opportunities for self-improvement.
20. **Personal relevance** – a job that provides me with opportunities to use my personal talents, education and training.
21. **Power** – a job that allows me to control my destiny and be influential.
22. **Promotion** – a job that provides opportunities for rapid advancement.
23. **Recognition** – a job that leads to clear and wide recognition of my achievements.
24. **Regularity** – a job that can be performed in a standard, stable and controlled manner.
25. **Responsibility** – a job with many appropriate responsibilities.
26. **Safety** – a job that can be carried out in safe and secure conditions.
27. **Security** – a job that is secure and permanent.
28. **Simplicity** – a job that is not overly-complicated.

29. **Social interaction** – a job that provides many good opportunities for social contact with others.
30. **Status** – a job that is generally recognized as "high-status" in our society.
31. **Stimulation** – a job that I personally find very interesting.
32. **Supervision** – a boss who is fair and considerate.
33. **Teaching** – a job that allows me to train others and to pass on my expertise.
34. **Teamwork** – a job that provides me with opportunities to cooperate with others.
35. **Tranquility** – a job that is not particularly stressful.
36. **Variety** – a job that allows me to be involved in many different kinds of activities.
37. **Visibility** – a job that gives me a fair amount of publicity.

All these things drive people, but some more than others. Can we profile individuals and therefore derive the motivational DNA of an individual person? Maybe. If so, what are the implications? A person's abilities and personality and values combine to determine the vocational choices they make and the training they select. Some are lucky: they have opportunities and make wise choices. Some have less happy experiences; partly through circumstances well beyond their control, partly because of their own lack of insight.

A parsimonious approach has been taken by Robert Hogan, who has developed a test of personal values. Based on the work of other researchers, it suggests that we all have a unique profile of the interests and values that shape and influence us. These are our drivers/motivators; this is what we seek in the workplace and, if it provides them, we are supposedly happy and productive.

Our attributes, personalities and values, which are all interconnected, predict the sort of employment training we seek out and the jobs we apply for. These, in turn, predict the sort of things that lead us to be happy or unhappy at work:

1. **Recognition** – desire to be known, seen, visible and famous, which leads to a lifestyle guided by a search for opportunities to be noticed and dreams of fame and high achievement, whether or not they are fulfilled.
2. **Power** – desire to succeed, make things happen, make a difference and outperform the competition.

3. **Hedonism** – pursuit of fun, excitement, pleasure and a lifestyle organized around eating, drinking and entertainment.
4. **Altruism** – desire to help others, a concern for the welfare of the less fortunate in life, and a lifestyle organized around public service and the betterment of humanity.
5. **Affiliation** – needing and enjoying frequent and varied social contact and a lifestyle organized around social interaction.
6. **Tradition** – a belief in, and dedication to, old-fashioned virtues such as family, church, thrift, hard work and appropriate social behavior, and a lifestyle that reflects these values.
7. **Security** – a need for predictability, structure and efforts to avoid risk and uncertainty (especially in the employment area) and a lifestyle organized around minimizing errors and mistakes.
8. **Commerce** – interest in earning money, realizing profits, finding new business opportunities, and a lifestyle organized around investments and financial planning.
9. **Aestheticism** – need for self-expression; a dedication to quality and excellence; an interest in how things look, feel and sound; and close attention to the appearance of things.
10. **Science** – being interested in science, comfortable with technology, preferring data-based (as opposed to intuitive) decisions, and spending time learning how things work.

The secret of a motivated individual by this definition is the round peg in the round hole – where the values, interests and passions of the individual are provided by the job. Of course, jobs change, as do organizations. The job can change around one, and this certainly affects motivation.

Managing in hard times

Do you have to manage differently in hard times, or simply better? Is turbulence not an excellent Darwinian mechanism to sort out those fit to manage from those who could get away with things during the bad times?
The first issue is to ask a few questions:

- How to react in ways that do not threaten long-term survival?
- How to ensure the organization can recognize, respond to, and exploit all opportunities thrown up by the turbulence?

- Are we using our time and energy most productively to ensure adaptation and survival?
- What difficult issues are we really avoiding, ignoring or repressing, to our cost?
- Do we have the moral and interpersonal courage to do the right thing?
- Who is most and least deserving of our staff, customers and suppliers to support, help and bolster?
- Are we modeling how we want our staff to behave?

Turbulence means often laying people off. People are not, then, a great asset but, rather, a great liability. Too often, managers look for easy or quick solutions in bad times. These typically include the following:

- Recruitment freezes – simply not taking on any more staff.
- Pay freezes, non-payment of increments, or pay-cuts – which can hurt a great deal.
- Pay deferral schemes, which are somewhat like pensions – when (if) the good times return, that is when the business can pay people.
- Removal or elimination of overtime that may have got out of hand.
- Reviewing temporary hire, agency and contract staff to see whether they can be cut, rather than core staff.
- A shorter working week/flexible working, so that people work less, but also get paid less.
- Cutting bonuses or reviewing other benefits for top people, or all people in the organization.
- Reviewing pension contributions and/or benefit levels to see whether they can be cut.
- Extended or additional (unpaid) annual leave to reduce costs.
- Offering unpaid or half-pay sabbaticals for long-serving staff.
- Offering "career breaks," where people, at their own cost, can take various breaks to pursue other activities.
- Trying secondments to other companies who are doing better.
- Redeployment in other parts of the business.

Each of these has legal implications and may simply not be possible. They are all aimed at reducing the pay bill, and may be a short-term solution only. Moves such as these can have both beneficial and deleterious consequences. Managers may discover they can work just as efficiently with fewer staff. Alternatively, there may be unforeseen implications that attempts to save money actually work out to be more expensive.

So, what else do managers need to do?

- Re-engage with staff, who are naturally anxious and worried, through frequent, consistent, honest communication – lunch-time workshops. Tell them the truth; listen to their concerns.
- Lead from the front: be seen and be strong, bold, adventurous. Don't hide away and make excuses not to see people who need support.
- Learn from previous recessions. Beware cutting that which adds customer value: easy things to cut can have terrible consequences that cost a great deal more in the long run. Don't go for big, publicity-seeking gestures unless they really work. Do the little things right.
- Fix the leaks that appear immediately. All sorts of things can happen in times of change. Monitor morale and finances and output carefully.
- Innovate: this maybe an ideal time to get creative with all the stakeholders. Leaders have even been known to try to bring about crises to ensure that people are more receptive to structural and people–policy change. Sharpen your focus, streamline your processes.
- Try to attract talent badly managed elsewhere. This maybe the best time to recruit really talented people from other organizations who are not managing the crisis well.
- Prepare for economic recovery. Make sure you are ready when the up-turn happens.

The central question is whether to manage well in hard times leaders have to do something **different** or simply manager **better**. The answer is the latter. The basic issues of management are the same for all organizations and at all times. It is just that in hard times, during a downturn and where there is turbulence, it is **all the more important**.

The central tasks of leading are:

Inspiring others: This includes everyone associated with the organization from shareholders and customers to the staff who work in it. The manager has to convince others that they understand the issues and what to do. He or she needs to inspire them to work harder, more efficiently, and smarter for the greater good of all. But inspiration is about the head and the heart: it is about responding to the emotions of others. It requires the combination of intellect *and* passion.

Having focus: This is about being able to distinguish the wheat from the chaff: about understanding what is crucial and what trivial; about how to use limited resources most effectively. It is about planning and organizing and keeping one's eye always on the ball … all the time. It is about keeping to path and the plan, though checking periodically whether this requires any revisions in the face of changing circumstances.

Enabling others: This is all about making sure that people are able to do what is required of them. That they have the right information, tools, and training; and that they know what is required of them. The need the tools (intellectual, emotional and skill-based) to do the job. This is more than delegation and the problems of over-controlling, micro-management. It is about having the strategy, structure, processes and values that allow people to do what is required of them and enjoy taking responsibility for their actions.

Reinforcing and rewarding others: We all need feedback on our performance. Feedback, like all rewards, comes in many types. It can be planned and scheduled or spontaneous. It can be simple or complex; detailed or superficial. And it can be tangible (in the form of money) or less tangible in the form of praise. Every parent, teacher and coach knows the power of positive feedback to sustain and direct good behavior. It is all the more important in difficult times.

Learning: There are many lessons in *experience*, which is why it is so valued. People who have experienced previous recessions and crises frequently (but not always) do better when faced with them again. This involves reflection and analysis; it is about using feedback and learning particularly from mistakes.

Not easy then; but not something very special. Managing in a downturn certainly tests the basic qualities of all managers.

1 Ability, aspiration, attitude

Essentially, you need three things to be (really) successful at work: ability, aspiration and attitude. Ability refers to intellect, talent, particular gifts. It's the size of the engine in the car. You also need to have real aspirations to succeed: to be driven, hungry and seriously motivated. This explains the direction of the car. And, you need the right attitude: these are traits and values such as perseverance, integrity and curiosity. This is the make or brand of the car.

It's difficult to fail or under-achieve with high scores for the whole set. The effortless ease of the talented, focused and adjusted individual is the "gift of the gods." Throw in good looks and health, and they are the natural wunderkinder of the world. Equally, it's impossible to succeed without the three essentials. Some are just dealt a bad hand – perhaps they chose their parents badly. To be a low-wattage, low-adjustment person born into a feckless family is clearly no great start in life.

What of those with two of the three core requirements? How about the able, aspiring and attitude-less? "Attitude," as the Americans say, "is everything." But what is it and can it be changed? Attitude comes from personality and values, which are linked and not that easy to change. Some people seem more aggressive than others; some more fragile. Clever, hungry but neurotic children may find it difficult to channel their ability easily. The able and aspiring may have come to expect that things occur too easily for them. Their attitude can alienate others. Ability can lead to hubris or superciliousness. Motivation, to extreme and damaging competitiveness.

How successful are the able with the right attitude but no drive? Drive or ambition or motivation is always the hard one. It is not that difficult to measure ability, or even attitudes. Life is an intelligence and personality test. By the time people are adults, we tend to have a great deal of data on these two. But what really motivates people? Indeed, can they tell us, or is it buried in some mysterious unconscious past? The drive for power or recognition? For admiration or social approval?

It's often sad to see talented individuals fritter away their talents. The brilliant scholar ending up in a dead-end career, never exploring or exploiting what they have been given. That smart school child who walked off with all the prizes but never seemed to follow it through. Ah, but perhaps that is the path of happiness. Maybe!

And those with ambition and attitude but lowish ability? Will their drive and personality profile carry them through? Often. It does depend on two things, of course – how low their ability, weak their talents, but also what they intend to do. Difficult to reach the top as a classical musician without talent? Perhaps less so as a pop star. All jobs now seem to carry a talent profile. Some require more verbal ability, others more mathematical ability. There are different forms of literacy that we pick up on. The talented pick them up fast and easily.

The adjusted and ambitious person with modest talent can easily thrive. This, in part, depends on their self-awareness and chosen path. The less talented but highly motivated (with the right attitude) might see that they simply have to work harder than their colleagues to achieve the same end. Their motivation compensates. And, to be frank, some jobs involve more talent than others. It's the ratio of perspiration to inspiration. For many careers, you need **enough** ability but, more than that, you need drive, hard work and the right attitude. Seriously short-changed people are probably clearly capped in terms of their prospects. But the low average can thrive, if they have the ambition and the drive to succeed.

Perhaps you have a fair chance with two factors out of the three, but one alone – sometimes it is difficult to imagine how that works. The genius with low ambition and the wrong attitude? Yep, the lives of artists are littered with stories of disturbed, easily-bruised and dejected people of great talent who are remembered for their genius so flickeringly revealed.

And the person with a sunny disposition and healthy values but less talent and drive? They can have indeed, often do have – happy and contented lives. Their attitude is appreciated. It makes for happy and healthy relationships at, and outside, work. They may readily find their niche in the caring professions or in some people-centered support role.

The saddest of all are those with an all-consuming ambition but little to fulfill it. The entitlement "bad attitude" can be deeply off-putting, particularly in combination with a clear lack of talent. This is, paradoxically, most likely to manifest in talent shows. What is it about some sadly, yet self-evidently, unattractive but talentless people that they think they have talent? The real shock is less about their rejection than their outrage at being told the self-evident truth.

So, for a happy life you need the right attitude: for a successful one, the drive. Both are made a great deal easier with a generous dollop of real talent.

2 The abnormal boss

How abnormal is your boss? Sick, perverted, mean, bullying? A psychopathic, narcissistic bully? Or unusually charming, empathic and supportive?

Whilst it is relatively easy to spot people who are distressed or acting bizarrely, it is much more difficult to define abnormality. Abnormal means "departure from the norm." For psychologists, the issue is not so much whether the behavior is abnormal, as whether it is maladaptive; causing a person distress and social impairment.

Early approaches to abnormality saw bizarre behavior as "spirit possession." Then people believed in animalism: the belief that we were very similar to animals and that madness was the result of uncontrolled regression. Ancient Greeks saw abnormality and general malaise caused by bodily fluids or "humors" (bile). As a result, early treatment of the insane mostly involved in segregating them and then punishing them. Humane treatment did not really appear until the nineteenth century.

There are various ways to define abnormality:

Subjective: this is perhaps the most primitive idea that uses ourselves, our behavior, our values as the criteria of normality. This is the stuff of idiom and adage ("Once a thief, always a thief;" "There's nowt so queer as folk"). So, people like us are normal; those are not. Individuals can have very strange personal theories of oddness, madness and strangeness based on personal experiences and values. They are often surprised to find how few share their opinions.

Normative: this is the idea that there is an ideal, desirable state of how one should think and behave. This view of the perfect world is often developed by religious and political thinkers. Normality is perfection: the further from normality one is, the more abnormal. It's more a "what ought to be" than "what is reasonably possible" state of affairs. Nothing is normal because nobody is perfect.

Cultural: culture dictates trends in everything from dress to demeanor, language to love. Culture prescribes and proscribes behaviors. Certain things are taboo; others are illegal. Again, the further away or different from cultural norms a person appears to be, the more he or she is judged as abnormal. However, as cultural beliefs and practices change, so do definitions of normality. In some cultures, bosses are expected to be authoritarians; in others, this would be taboo.

Statistical: all statisticians know the concept of the bell curve or the normal distribution. It has particular properties and is best-known in the world of intelligence. Thus, a score of 100 is average; 66 percent of the population score between 85 and 115, and around 97 percent between 70 and 130. Thus, if you score below 70 and more than 130, you are unusual: extreme, though the word "abnormal" would not be applied.

Clinical: social science and medical clinicians attempt to assess the effectiveness, organization and adaptiveness of a person's functioning. Much depends on which dimension is being assessed. Clinicians also accept that the normal–abnormal distinctions are grey and somewhat subjective, though they strive for reliable diagnosis.

Psychological definitions of abnormality revolve around half a dozen or so "generally agreed upon" criteria. These have been called the 4Ds: distress, deviance, dysfunction, danger. Abnormality generally involves pain and suffering. Acute and chronic personal suffering is one criterion. Another is poor adaptation – not being able to do the everyday things of life, such as hold down a job, maintain happy interpersonal relationships, and plan for the future.

A very common criterion is irrationality – having bizarre, illogical beliefs about the physical or social world as well, as very often, the spiritual world. Irrational behavior is often incomprehensible to others. Abnormal people are often unpredictable; they can be very volatile, changing from one extreme to another and often quite unable to control their behavior. Their behavior is often very inappropriate.

Almost by definition, their abnormality is characterized by unconventional, rare, usually undesirable behaviors. It is sometimes called "vivid" and "eccentric." In addition, abnormality has a moral dimension. It is associated with breaking rules, violating moral standards, disregarding social norms. Illegal, immoral, undesirable behavior is abnormal.

There is one other rather interesting criterion of abnormality. It's the discomfort that is generated in people around abnormality. Observers – be they friends, family or just onlookers – often feel uncomfortable around clear evidence of abnormality.

There are at least three problems of the concept of normality. *First*, a healthy person in an unhealthy society is often labeled as abnormal. There have been many historical incidents where sick societies have been deeply intolerant of those who don't obey or concur with their narrow (unhealthy, maladaptive) standards of belief and behavior.

Second, of course, expert observers can't agree on the categorization of normal vs. abnormal. Even when multiple criteria of abnormality are specified, there remains fundamental disagreement about whether a person is considered, in some sense, abnormal.

Third, there is the actor–observer difference: who is to make the judgment? "Actors" rarely think themselves abnormal: most of us are reasonably positive about ourselves and, indeed, have a great deal of information others do not have. Yet, there are well-known traps and hazards in making a self-diagnosis. It is easier to be observers and label others abnormal, particularly those different from us or threatening to us.

Extremes of normality are abnormality. The extreme extrovert may be manic or prone to hysteria; the extremely conscientious person, a touch obsessional and perfectionistic. The cuddly, agreeable boss may be "too soft with people," and the highly stable and adjusted boss unable to understand stress in others. Nothing wrong with being normal.

3 Achieving staff engagement

Once it was called "work satisfaction," then "job commitment" and now "engagement." Its opposite is called "alienation:" estranged, from all that happens in the workplace.

Engagement matters, because it directly affects the bottom line. To some extent, engagement is another word for "morale." When it exists high absenteeism, theft and turnover goes down and productivity and customer satisfaction goes up. Good leadership creates engagement; bad management destroys it – quickly and devastatingly. There is engagement of the head, and of the heart.

All managers want their staff fully committed to the aims of the organization, happy in their work and totally engaged in what they are doing. So, how to achieve it? Indeed, is it possible to engage people doing unskilled, dreary, repetitive work? And is engagement an end in itself, or does it lead to all those desirable things like productivity, profitability, retention and customer satisfaction?

The research in this area shows fairly consistent findings. The results are neither surprising nor counter-intuitive. And they have been known for ages. So, why is it that supervisors and managers do not perform their duties so as to maximize the commitment and engagement of their staff?

There are some pretty basic but important things one needs to do to maximize engagement. They are a check list – Management 101:

- Let every person know what is expected of them in terms of their processes and products. Be clear. Check understandings. And revisit expectations as they change. All people have hopes and expectations about promotion, about development, about what their organization should be doing for them (and what they should be doing for the organization). These people need to be managed.
- Give people the tools for the job: keep them up-to-date and train people how to use them. Make sure that processes are well thought through, so that the technology people use is appropriate for what they are required to do. In short, give technical and informational support.

- Give people opportunities to learn and shine at what they are good at. People like to celebrate their skills, abilities and unique gifts. Help them find and explore them. Let them do their best all the time. And encourage development of personal strengths.
- Be generous, but targeted, in praise. Recognize effort and success. Recognize individuals and how they strive to achieve. Celebrate success. Notice and praise individuals when they have put in extra effort. And do it openly, naturally and regularly.
- Listen to your employees. They often have very good innovative ideas. Yes, they can and do complain, but listen to that too. They need to believe their ideas count, their voice is heard, that they can contribute to how the work is arranged. Loss of autonomy and control and voice are deeply alienating.
- Help them believe in the purpose or product of the organization. People need to feel their job is important; that they are really making a contribution to society. This involves more than writing fancy mission statements. It's about giving the job a sense of meaning and purpose for all employed.
- Encourage formation of friendships at work. This is more than insisting on team work. It is giving people space and time to build up a friendship network. Friends are a major source of social support – and enemies create social stress. Friends make all the difference to the working day. And committed people commit to their friends.
- Talk to people about their progress. Give them a chance to let off steam; to dream about what might be; to have quality time with you. This is more than those detailed – often, rather forced – bureaucratic appraisals. It is about opportunity for the boss to focus on the hopes, aspirations and plans of the individual.

Pretty obvious stuff. Be clear about what you want. That is, define the outcomes required for individuals and challenge them to stretch themselves. Focus on what they do well: their strengths, gifts and talents. Try to find the best individual and the best in the individual. Make them exemplars, heroes, models. Find the right fit between a person's talents and ambitions and the tasks they need to do.

Look for ambitious, achievement-oriented, energetic individuals. But steer their striving: manage their route-map. And look for, listen to and reward evidence of independent ideas and innovative thinking. Never

assume management has a monopoly on the truth. Also, encourage cama-
raderie: help people who are social animals relate to each other and pull
together.

Do all of the above and you'll have an engaged workforce. And we do
know happy, healthy, staff treat customers better and generate the profit.
It's a relatively simple causal link. It pays to focus on staff engagement.
But it's also the fundamental task of all management.

4 The annual company conference

Many organizations have an annual conference, though they take rather different forms and happen for different reasons. They can cost a great deal: but what is their function and what are the alternatives? Would a works-outing be a more useful replacement? Who should be involved? How do you measure the success of these occasions?

Some organizations prefer a quasi-shareholders meeting. There is a "state-of-the-nation" address, followed by department heads doing their stuff. It's all very cerebral but with sexed-up slides, "vox pop" video clips and possibly party bags. These conferences are curious mixtures of serious and frivolous appeal. They are there primarily to inform, but also to thank and inspire. Mostly, they involve passive audiences with the occasional "on your table" discussions. Hence the cabaret lay out.

Depending on the venue and the support staff required, these conferences can be extremely expensive. They need set designers and audio-visual specialists. They may employ graphic artists, even lighting specialists; though there are now companies who offer the whole package. And times are hard.

There has clearly been inflation in conferencing. The school hall, the dais and the company motto or shield just won't do. Many people attend conferences, conventions, seminars, workshops, and so on, and they have come to expect the stagecraft of it all. Conference companies are very sensitive to the required theatricality. Indeed, their staff are often part-timers who are "something" in theatre. They dress only in black; some have ponytails to prove they are creative.

They look for the "wow factor" as people enter the room: lighting, music, tinsel are all there to create maximum effect. And it changes when the CEO runs (that part is compulsory, because he must look both fit and enthusiastic) onto the stage. Some still have a fanfare of trumpets.

The next consideration after the venue, the staging and so forth is whether to have a guest speaker. Many bureaus offer the service of celebrities great and small. For a price, you can have famous sporting or television stars, politicians, writers or comedians. They come at a price where, by and large, market forces work: more famous, more money. Even old "has been" dubious actors and politicians can command a pretty penny.

What about motivational speakers? The person who can add the "can do attitude," the "buzz," the "pizzazz" to the conference. Apart from the cost, is there a risk? What if they disappoint? What if they so upstage the CEO that he or she looks incoherent and inarticulate? What if all the delegates can remember two weeks later are a few well prepared quips from motivational speakers' scripts? Then, consider a famous "chair-person" who pops up throughout the day to introduce, thank, quiz or summarize. They perform a sort of bookend function, as well by starting and ending the conference on a high point. Good idea – but a great deal more money.

Conferences where the delegates are talked at, and presented to, often turn into a "death by PowerPoint" affair. There is only so much that people can absorb. So, what about activities: should they be round-table and "meaningful;" or more like fun and games with a quiz, a treasure hunt or some sporting activities?

And there is yet more to worry about. What about lunch – buffet or silver service, with or without booze, short or long? Certainly, one thing professional conference organizers do know is that if you screw up the lunch, you are finished. Lunch is tangible: cut corners at your cost. Booze is no longer common, but don't make people queue for a local deli-spread of sandwiches. And remember that networking occurs during the breaks. It is part of the aim of the conference.

How should the conference end? What about party bags? A surprise star-turn? The singing of the company hymns? The primacy–recency effect clearly shows that people remember more from the beginning and from the end than anything in the middle of the event. So, create a strong impression and let them go with the message ringing in their ears. But there's the rub. What is the message or the purpose of the conference? What can an organization realistically achieve at such an event? Why hold them annually? Would the money not be more usefully spent on a day-trip to Paris on Eurostar, a family day at Center Parcs or a day off for all employees?

It is important to clarify the purpose of the conference in order to judge its efficiency or justify its costs. If all you want is for people to have a good time and feel thanked for their contributions, the issue is much simpler. If you want them to understand the necessity for the restructuring or the merger and acquisition, that is another issue. If you want to signpost to the media the health of the company, this, again, is a different issue. Form follows function.

It may be a useful start to ask staff what events that they went to that they enjoyed and those that bored them stiff. And, of course, what they remembered; or, harder still, what real behavior change resulted.

5 Anti-management ideas on management apologetics

There is a branch of theology called "Apologetics." It not about being contrite, guilty and chanting eternally "*mea culpa.*" It is about providing a systematically reasoned argument in defense and vindication of (Christian) beliefs. An apologist is, therefore, one who speaks and writes in defense of a belief system, specific cause or institution.

For some time, it has been fashionable to be anti-management. This is the conventional argument: most organizations would be a great deal better off with fewer managers. After all, most simply inhibit and frustrate those doing real work in production and sales. Further, management is not a profession, just the commonsensical following of intuition and, where that fails, the calling in of consultants. Disillusionment with managers seen to be a lethal mixture of corrupt and incompetent results either in the imposition of more legislation to try to ensure standards are maintained, or else the use of the executive as a watch dog. Worse, get shareholders to try the job of management. These solutions nearly always end in tears.

It is said that managers are, too often, slow, bureaucratic, hierarchical, inflexible and inadaptable. Elephantine megaliths, the natural home of the middle-managers, are as doomed as a Dilbert Dodo. The fleet-footed, high-tech, high-touch, highly-adaptable firms are the world of tomorrow. The new employee is a self-managing, portfolio-oriented, multi-talented person in no need of a middle-brow, controlling middle manager. Right?

So, how to defend the indefensible?

Defense 1: Large companies not only persist, but increase. Car, insurance, publishing and pharmaceutical companies are growing larger, not smaller. Governments start quangos to try to prevent megalithic monopolies. Few succeed in so doing.

Companies get bigger because of the advantage of economies of scale. When companies have tens of thousands of employees, someone has to define, direct and co-ordinate, particularly where standardization is thought to be important. In fact, the increase in managers is usually modest relative to the increase in the number of employees. And, as all armies from all nations for all time have discovered, things like a **clear chain of**

command with a realistic **span of control** and **logical procedures** simply provides the best way to get things done.

Defense 2: Small companies need managers. Whilst entrepreneurial owners are seeking out opportunities, sourcing finance, negotiating contracts, someone has to keep the show on the road. Someone has to do the payroll and taxes, order stocks and comply with legal requirements. Those who let go the "hands-on bit" often see the company stall: but to grow means letting go … to the appropriate middle-manager. In fact, we have known for 50 years that small companies tend to have proportionately more managers than larger ones. It's that economy vs. scale argument again.

Defense 3: As the business world becomes more complex – and, therefore, more difficult to administer – there are more, rather than fewer, needs for managerial expertise. Increases in regulation, consumer pressure groups, and economic instability require more managerial expertise. A good manager is a tactician, a stabilizer, a morale-booster, and so on. We all need less regulation and better managers.

Defense 4: Managers are better-educated today than they ever were. Sure, some revel in jargon; others follow fads; some are dogmatic – but they are, for the most part, better trained. Management might not be a profession in the established sense of the word, but there is evidence that general managers are better-educated than they have ever been.

There is nothing wrong with structure: structures are organizing principles; media of communication; lives of report. They need to fit the product, the culture, the times. They can be changed. But only the fool (or management guru) wants to be structure-less. That is clearly the route to anarchy.

Perhaps the greatest culprit in the demise of the status of the manager is the block-buster business book written by the quasi-academic guru. Management is portrayed as simple: follow a few simple points and you become a great manager. Walk about; throw a few fish about; move your cheese or whatever.

Have the management-bashers all their own way? Business schools try valiant defense by their apologists that looks as if it is based as much on reputation and greed as anything else.

The public often sees managers as corrupt, obsessed, naïve or plain lazy. They are less often portrayed as people wrestling with complex problems in a volatile environment. They tried to cull a generation of middle-managers during the downsizing fad or re-engineering. It led to tears and capsizing, not right-sizing.

No amount of spin or PR can save managers their respect or reputation. They have to make serious decisions in the face of uncertainty; they have to separate signal from noise in the data; they have to boost and sustain morale; they have to create a culture of success … blah, blah.

Managers need to be taught to articulate their role and contribution in a non-defensive way. They need to look and be up-to-speed, and be thoughtful and able to communicate in jargon-free language. In short, they need to act like any other professional.

The processes of classical management are not out-of-date anymore than are those of parenting. Managers need their apologists in times of unprecedented criticism. Perhaps "Management Apologetics" should be top of the curriculum at all good business schools.

6 Blind dates and speed dating

It has been suggested that speed dating was invented by an American Rabbi interested in helping Los Angeles Jews meet each other. "Customers" had 10–25 four-minute dates, after which they had a binary question: yes or no. Two yeses meant a date and a more traditional meeting was arranged.

It caught on. Much better (certainly shorter) than blind dates. In speed dating, both parties declare themselves interested in meeting a romantic partner. Better, both can give unambiguous feedback on their perceptions without having to do so face-to-face. Rather than too hasty, they could be described as mercifully brief. Devout Muslims adapted the procedure. Yes, they have parental chaperones and they don't call it speed dating, but that is what it is.

Blind dates can be wonderful, as well as total hell. It depends on who arranges them and can very easily lead to the end of a great friendship. They are a bit like receiving rather odd presents where, quite clearly, the giver shows that he or she really does not understand your taste, values or likes.

Blind dates can, thankfully, be short and structured. A dinner dance is all over in four to five hours and one may part happily with a feeling of "Let's chalk that up to experience." On the other hand, blind dates can afford wonderful and unique opportunities to meet people that one is unlikely to come across in everyday life.

Scientists insist on double-blind, randomized, controlled trials to provide a real test of the efficacy of drugs. It means people are randomly assigned to two or more groups, one of which is on a sugar pill placebo: the control group. The double-blind means neither the doctor nor the patient knows whether they are getting the "real thing" (i.e. the experimental drug) or the placebo.

More blind dates are double-blinded. Neither knows who they are getting or why. This is usually the meddling of a well-intended if, alas all too often, emotionally intelligent friend. On the other hand, arranged marriages are very carefully planned. Societies that promote arranged marriages see marriage as a deal between families. It is a sort of merger and acquisition arrangement, where one (minor) dynasty marries into another. The aim is synergy and heirs; stability and longevity of the lineage. Whether the people love one another – or, indeed, grow to do so – is really beside the point.

Farmers "mate" animals. Some kindly, middle-class people attempt to mate their friends at drinks and dinner parties.

Speed dating, however, is different. It is perfectly geared up to the fast consumerist world of young professionals. Further, it can be "scientifically" justified by research that is called "thin slices" or "zero acquaintance." The data show that, having accurately measured an individual's abilities and personality, an observer can (relatively) accurately judge these based on an interview of less than a minute or a video clip of the person talking about themselves for less than 10 seconds.

There are now "speed dating scholars," because of the opportunities this activity provides to study relationships. If 20 men and 20 women attend a speed dating evening, it might result in 400 "dyadic" interactions. So, they have structured reciprocity, which is the extent to which people who desire either a specific individual or various others are desired in return. They have also studied how their very brief interactions (which are recorded) predict all sorts of behavior, from emails to marriage, after the event.

Some results are known before they emerge: men go for attractiveness, women for earnings. But they also found evidence for chemistry because, if you ask people beforehand what they are looking for (ideal or optimal characteristics) and then observe how they rate real people, they are not the same. People lack insight or tell "porkie-pies." They seem to be unable to say why they choose who they do.

People base judgments more on what they can easily see (i.e. physical features) than by less observable characteristics such as education or the desire to have children. But values do count.

So, is it better to meet someone at a church social over the water cooler or on the beach, rather than at a speed dating event? Which leads to finding a better-quality, longer-lasting relationship? Are those who (dare to) take up speed dating somehow different from those that don't?

And what are the best questions to ask in your allotted time? And what to look for as best indicators of what you are after?

Finally, beware: it is unlikely that there are hidden cameras or microphones in the room, but it would not be that unusual if the person you are trying so enthusiastically to chat up is actually a social scientist doing a PhD on Darwinianly-inspired mate selection.

7 Bridge employment

Remember the 1980s? Greed is good! Make your (serious) pile by 40, then retire. An endless life of golf tournaments, Caribbean holidays, shopping trips to warm countries with weak currencies A vision of heaven … or hell?

Now it seems that the big bang boomers did not retire as they planned. It was not so much that they failed at their business, or even that "Black Wednesday" blew a massive hole in their portfolio. Rather, they changed their goals. Somehow their target goal seemed too modest. Once you had three million ($, £ or €), you saw how little it really was.

Also, they feared getting out of the loop. Business gives a buzz. Yes, there is stress, demand, frustration. But it is also really exciting. You meet interesting people; go to interesting places; your ideas and opinions are (apparently) taken seriously.

It is for this reason that many high- (and low-) powered people find retiring difficult. Some do "close the door," happily pottering around until the Grim Reaper calls. Yet, many hate it – mostly men, particularly those "forced" to retire at a certain age or because they are made redundant.

So, what are the options for those retirees who are not satisfied with the pipe and potting shed, the slippers and sedentary pursuits? It seems around 15 million Americans and around 3 to 4 million Britons opt to remain in the workforce in some capacity. How many over the age of 65 are in full-time employment is unclear.

A new concept describes this phenomenon. It's called **bridge employment**. It means the work (full- or part-time, temporary or self-employment) that bridges between a "real" career job and real (employment-less) retirement. It's a trade-off between reduced wages and status and flexibility.

There are two types: career and non-career bridge employment. The former means staying in the same job or organization, but opting for different conditions. The latter means doing something potentially quite different in a different place for a different organization.

Bridge employment may mean staying – in the same company or job sector – but doing less for less. A quieter, less stressful but less monetarily-rewarded life. The non-career bridge is trying something new: job, sector, function. Or, of course, there remains the real option of complete full unemployment.

So, it's a choice. Disengagement or continuity amid change. People remain much the same, whatever bridge they cross. Same attitudes and inclinations; same likes and dislikes. Same sense of who you are; what you stand for.

What predicts the choices people coming up for retirement make? An obvious one is what might be called "career attachment" – how committed an individual was to the job before the age-related marker happened. The more the attachment, the more the bridge option is chosen. The more attached to the job, the career, the company, the more one wants to stay. But there are other factors. The more stress and strain associated with the pre-retirement job, the more attractive full-time unemployment.

Next, the more intrinsically, rather than extrinsically, satisfying the job, the more people want to stay. If they have autonomy, identify with the task and the company, and use their skills, they like to stay on.

Further, there is the pull, the nostalgia of work-related accomplishments. The more successful people have been in achieving their goals, the more acute their exit consciousness and the more likely they are to seek a bridge.

And related to that is the personal skill set. Some skills are highly job-specific, others general. Mathematics skills and a good vocabulary are useful everywhere, whilst tap-dancing and welding are less transferable. So, the more specific the skill that indicates high IQ, the easier to find a career bridge job.

The bottom line? Many people feel too young, fit and healthy to retire. They know work has benefits. So, many seek out part-time or simply less-demanding work. And what predicts where and what sort of job they look for? Some want continuity and others change; some are happy to close the door on a long-term career and try to get another. This choice depends mainly on things such as career history and skills.

Sour, alienated under-achievers certainly don't seek out bridge employment. In fact, they are not likely to seek out employment at all. Carriers of gloom and dissatisfaction, they are best suited to the old-fashioned view of the retiree.

8 Business and the media

It is remarkable how quickly people and their companies rise and fall in popularity. One day a wunderkind, a hero, a chosen one and the next, a shallow, dubious, charlatan. Is it a northern hemisphere manifestation of the tall poppy syndrome? Is it poor judgment, or the demands of the modern public that we place artistic, business and potential leaders on a pedestal then tear them down.

The relationship between the media and top politicians and business leaders is certainly complex. They need each other, but it is a bit like a three-legged race on the quick-sand of business.

Politicians, business bosses and stars of all sorts can't control the media as they can those who work for them. But they see good (and bad) press as extremely important to their future. So, they court the media: the charm offensive begins. They use the familiar bag of tricks open to those in the business of advertising and selling. Flattery, gifts, special offers and relationships: and some of it works.

And reporters obtain that most valuable of assets: access. Favorite media people become "one-of-us." Not exactly on the payroll, but a "good friend" and "confidante" of the great-and-the-(often not so)-good.

But journalists are meant to be fearless, objective and disinterested need-to-know people. So, if they write an insightful and critical piece about a person or a company, they are punished by having their access withdrawn. It is as though, quite suddenly, their swipe card no longer works. The coward's way of sacking people.

Even worse, in some cases, the word gets out to a whole group of individuals: "Don't talk to X." Doors are closed, phone messages remain unanswered: even the little people (read security and support staff) will not engage.

So, what does our investigative reporter do? He or she has to rely on the opponents of the person or organization, which leads to increased criticism and the chance of access slipping even further away.

But good PR is essential. Top business leaders are invited onto television programs – some jolly and banal, others hard-hitting – and are fearlessly and intelligently quizzed by fine assertive minds. So, wise politicians and companies employ people whose job it is to court the media. Some reporters are "favored." They are drip-fed exclusive "sound bites" about the issue in which they are interested.

Many business leaders are very susceptible to good PR: to shots of themselves with great celebrities. Check out their offices next time for the photographs. It feeds their self-esteem, often to the point of clinical narcissism. To have a tame journalist who does *Hello* magazine positive interviews is a god-send to any big businessman and company.

One reason why business leaders seem particularly interested in the media is that often journalists try to "sex up" what they see to be very dry news about pork-belly futures, oil barrel prices or complex tax changes by adding "people interest." The human face behind the news sells the news.

Some journalists, indeed, specialize in leadership profiles, mini-biographies, bordering on the hagiographic. This can lead to a very unhealthy relationship. The starred leader falls prey to the symptom of Narcissistic Personality Disorder, whilst the journalist turns into something between a myopic groupie and a lay psychoanalyst.

The British like sniping at pomposity. But it does seem odd that they seem to spend an equal amount of time and effort first building up a leader, only then to try to knock them down. Grow a tall poppy, then prune it viciously. Rising stars become fallen angels. They dramatically move either up or down. The hard-working, highly competent leader is not news.

Is it possible that the media cause – or, at least, provoke – management derailment? Can they intoxicate a person – which, over time, leads to tox-icity? Certainly, both good and bad media attention can easily divert the attention of leaders, causing poor decision-making.

Whilst some leaders do, indeed, have to court the media, others are famously reclusive. Your preferences as a shareholder? The "often-in-the spotlight" leader who gets both good and bad press, or the retiring recluse? Is all publicity good publicity? Alas, there is no research to provide the answer.

9 Changeability, malleability and adaptability

One of the most contended and politically hot questions at the centre of people management is the issue of change and development. This is a left–right, sociological–biological, optimist–pessimist debate. It is one that raises much passion, because it touches fundamental values and beliefs, and also because it has wide-ranging implications in business.

On the one side stand the incrementalists: the "can do" people who think that everything is possible. They espouse the optimism of the ideology that everything can change (easily). Progress is possible: most things are possible. They believe in training, mentoring and coaching to improve attitudes, self-perceptions and skills. They are happy with counseling and therapy. In their view, we can all change for the better: learn new skills, and overcome personal problems and drawbacks.

So, they put money into training at work. They feel not only that they can up-skill people, but also change their attitudes and values. People can be taught to be emotionally intelligent, hard-working and honest. We all have talents, we are all creative … and we can be taught how to find, liberate, unblock and reveal those talents. All it takes is the time and the effort … and (of course) the money.

People, on this side of the continuum, consider that we are, to a large extent, products of our surroundings and environment. We are, or are not, enterprising, moral or motivated as a function (almost exclusively) of our situations in life. And this can change. We can "enrich" environments, and therefore enrich people. We can undo that which has been done and re-package people. There is always the possibility of redemption.

They banish the "negative" ideas of accepting what we have "been given" in the lottery of life. Not for them stoicism and acceptance. That is fatalist talk, they say. We can change all aspects of our lives – if we want to. Suffering is optional.

Some people believe we are all (potentially) talented: all-creative, all-intelligent leaders. We just need this talent to be tickled, released, unfettered. There are numerous "case studies" and books in the "slum-dog millionaire" mold that tell the story so well. And so, it is a story we love to hear: it is a story of hope. It is a saga of progress, of improvement. It sells well everywhere.

And this line of thinking supports much industry, inside and outside organizations. Consider training and development costs. Of course, you can't expect someone to be a pilot or a surgeon without considerable training. But don't they need some very special abilities or gifts in the first place? This is all about **personal** development and **management** training. It is about transformation from where we are to a new and better place.

There are differences, of course, in this (rag-tag) group of believers. Some are a little less hopeful than others that we can all change for the good. But there is such a huge change-industry that they support each other for economic reasons.

On the other side of the continuum are people who often like to think of themselves as "hard-headed realists." They are the entity-theorists: essentialists, if you like the philosophic terminology. These are from the "what you see is what you get" school of life. In their number are stoics, cynics and skeptics.

They are not all tough-minded eugenicists, socio-biologists and geneticists who seem to imply so much behavior is inherited. The Jesuits and the Freudians fall into this camp, at least for people at work. They may have been malleable as young children, but their upbringing has molded, shaped and formed them. Change is difficult: painful, protracted and limited.

So, in the world of work, they argue, it is pretty pointless wasting time and effort on coaching, development and training. It doesn't work very well. Look around you. That nerdy IT boffin's emotional intelligence course; that choleric finance manager's presentation skills course; that histrionic marketing manager's financial literacy course. Any change there then?

So, the obvious implication is to put your money into better selection. Find the right people in the beginning. Choose right: you can't change them later. The bride at the wedding dreams "I'll alter him," whilst she would be better off believing "aisle, altar, hymn."

To what extent do people move from one side of this debate to the other? Much common wisdom suggests we might shift our views – the old adage that youths have broad minds and narrow waists, and the middle-aged about the opposite. Equally, there is the line that goes "If you are not a socialist when young, you have no heart; if you are a socialist when old, you have no head."

Does the bitter pill of disappointment make optimists into pessimists? Knowing people for years, going to school reunions, even contacting them on *Facebook* must convince people how little we change Surely? Maybe not. We get wider, greyer and more wrinkly, but do we change our preferences and abilities? Do extroverts become introverts, the creative less so, and the dim suddenly bright?

The trouble is, pessimism doesn't sell. We all love the story of hope, redemption and change. Mending your ways, moving on, finding and discovering your potential. The desert plant's reaction to rain. Stories of conquering disability, misfortune and disaster. Indeed. But are there exceptions that prove the rule. As rare as miracles … and as disputed.

Perhaps the optimists are paradoxically right. We do change and are capable of great change but, alas, that change is to pessimism!

10　City survivor's guilt

War scars the living and the dead. It is often amazing to see tough old survivors of battles long ago, chokingly and tearfully recounting their story. Even more poignant is to watch them kneel before graves or stroke a memorial with the names of their fallen comrades.

Survivors' guilt is a well-established psychiatric condition in warfare. Soldiers know that who lives and dies is pretty random: certainly, it is very unpredictable. And some "cop it," whilst others don't. "Why me?" some ask.

And so it is in a time of cuts. There are dark clouds gathering and ominous warnings about deep cuts. People are going to be laid off in very large numbers. The lawyers are working hard. They know all the things that need to be done: clear criteria, with supported evidence, for why some people and not others. They know they need the "paper trail," and that they need to consult with the unions and employees' representatives.

Letting people go is an important skill. It needs to be done with tact, to ensure dignity and respect for all. The "messengers" need tact and clarity. They know they need to separate the person from the problem (it is the job, not the employee, that is being made redundant). They need to be very clear, open and straight-forward about the decision: no mixed, vague, pill-sugared messages. No comfortable euphemisms, no apologies or defenses. Say it and shut up: and expect a shock response. Normalize and validate that response. Don't rush it: provide support.

But the problem may not be with those that go: it is more with the survivors. Many wonder about the criteria for being "let go." Are they next? Was it just…? Were they treated fairly and with dignity?

Paradoxically, the survivors are ignored. They are expected to be grateful and ever-more hard-working to prove the choice of those that wield the axe and make the chops.

Most people like to believe that they live in a just, orderly and stable world where good wins out in the end. Hollywood knows this well. The good guys win over the baddies and live happily-ever-after. That is how it should be.

But what if things really are random? Counselors and therapists talk about the grief process and grief stages. They know that those in shock experience a wide range of beliefs, often in a set order. Numbness, depression, anger, guilt and so on. Therapists talk of a U-curve, such that things get gradually worse but then improve. The depth and length of the U-curve describes many things: the nature of the trauma; the resilience of the individual.

There are two interesting features of the grieving literature. The *first* is the presence of anger. Victims of misfortune rail against many things: God, other people (particularly politicians and senior managers), the injustice of it all. It's hard to counsel people when they are angry. But it's a natural phase, and can be both anticipated and dealt with.

The *second*, even more interesting feature of this literature is that the grieving and the dying often go though the same process. Equally, the unscathed survivor may experience as much trauma as the deeply hurt and the badly injured. It's popular now to talk about post-traumatic stress disorder. The idea is that, after a trauma – sometimes, quite a bit later – people begin to suffer all sorts of stress reactions. Panic attacks, sleeplessness, loss of appetite, flashbacks. This certainly does happen to people.

But what about the trauma of things happening to others, rather than oneself? What is it like to walk unscathed from a mangled car or plane wreck, bodies scattered around? What is it like to be the sole survivor of a shipwreck or a terrorist attack? Surely, much worse to survive a lay-off program! No comparison … in fact, even a pleasure to see that surly engineer or bolshy IT person get the flack!

But there are interesting and potentially subtle differences for city survivor guilt. The *first* is that the guilt is often made worse by the fact that those that are saved (stay) get promoted. Curiously, the survivor in the city can benefit from the job loss of others by their promotion. This can exacerbate the guilt. *Second*, and to make the first point worse, one may find oneself socializing with, even counseling, those who were let go and are the cause of the guilt. After all, many were close friends. So, on a regular basis, one meets old colleagues who were let go. Some adjust well, even feel liberated; but others become angry, apathetic or depressed. That, of course, increases the guilt. And this is why they tend to get shunned or forgotten.

Not an easy situation to deal with, whether you are a sacker, a sackee or a survivor. But recognizing that the problem exists is a useful start.

11 Cock-ups and cover-ups at work

We all make them: the cock-up at work. The un- or poorly proof-read report, full of errors; the clumsy, embarrassing presentation; the appraisal that leads to serious litigation; the insulted and pissed-off (very important) client. You get asked fundamental questions and you don't know the answer. Your facts are out-of-date, or wrong. You deliver late without warning, and not what you promised. Like death and taxes and all that, these things happen; they are clearly inevitable at some time.

But perhaps the way we respond to these inevitable set-backs is really telling. For most people, the obvious strategy is the apportioning of blame elsewhere … what we psychologists call **external attributions** or **defensive projections**. "It wasn't my fault governor!" "I was only following orders." "The information did not come through in time." The cock-up, we assert, lay not with ourselves but lazy colleagues, impulsive support staff or poor instructions. It was due to the cut-backs; the old technology; the bureaucratic systems and processes.

It could be due to the room being too hot (or cold, or stuffy), or the new computer system's teething problems. It is easy – and, for others, natural – to blame others, situations or systems. The problems could be caused by HR or IT policy, or systems. It's a bit more tricky blaming the boss but, for some, this may be the last resort. A bully, or harasser, or incompetent, or psychopath … your choice.

Another strategy is to blame it on some uncontrollable malady: a bad cold, a disorder or some other problem over which one has no control. Different organizations in different sectors seem to have different preferred types of excuses.

This externalizing maybe common, but it is not reassuring for a boss. There are a number of steps to be taken after a cock-up:

Step 1 is to own up. The errors, problems and failures were (and are) a big issue for you, the department and the organization. No minimization. You are shamed and embarrassed. You are the primary cause. The buck stops with you. "Alright gov, it's a fair cop." Yes, there were other factors that influenced the situation. And yes, you are not superhuman. But this is Step 1.

Step 2 is to be honest, own up, and take personal responsibility. Yes, it was (mainly) your fault. You are embarrassed; you do regret your actions or lack thereof. You let many people down. *Mea culpa.* Sincere enough … but not histrionic or overblown. You understand what has happened, who was at fault and what the consequences were.

Step 3 is more important. It is to attempt to ensure that it will not happen again … or, at least, not too frequently. The question is what you will do differently. If it's proof-reading, you will do it earlier and give it to a colleague. If it is the presentation, it means preparing and practicing. Same for appraisal. You may nominate yourself to go on a course … self-funded, as penance. You might even ask to know who the best person in the organization is at doing the task you got wrong or cocked up. You may want to ask to watch, observe and shadow them. This is often about correctly diagnosing the real cause of the problem and then dealing with the attribution.

Step 4 is to do what you say; to try again and to do better. You have to show you were serious in your efforts to see that the situation will not occur again. And it may be that you discover that, for various reasons, you may very well see the problem re-occur. It may be that your talents lie elsewhere; your natural preferences mean you are likely to see the problem repeat. So, the action may not be training or coaching or attempting a life change. It may be appointing someone to do the job better than you do it: to outsource some function. It may be to change processes or procedures that really don't work for you. Or it may be to consider that the job is not for you.

It is true that we can, and should, learn from our mistakes. We learn about ourselves and what we need to do differently. We know from the service recovery business that, paradoxically, people are more loyal to a brand or service if a cock-up occurs but is quickly put right or recovered. This is not a license to encourage cock-ups. It is, however, a good indicator that personal or process cock-ups can provide a unique opportunity to learn and improve one's image.

12 Communicate, communicate, communicate

Now more than ever, in these bear-market, double-dip, depression days, people want to hear from their boss, the CEO, the chairman of the board. They are worried, anxious and bewildered. Where will the axe fall? What is the future of the company? Will I still have a job by the end of the year? Now is the time for talking. More than that, it is the time for serious speech-making, to people who need reassurance, a direction, hope for the future. So, what should be the message? Get the image right.

First, **remain steady and calm under fire**. The confident CEO needs, most of all, to project that he or she is not stressed or rattled. This is the "we can take it," "we will survive," "we will come through all this fitter and stronger." "Be not afraid: we can weather the storm; we all need to be resilient, focused and determined, and we can win out." Give confidence to others.

Second, **be defiant** and **vigilant**. "We will not succumb or give in to the forces of darkness." This is the moral crusade bit. We are tough and resolved.

Third, **be fit in body and mind**. Fit for the challenge, fit for the journey. This is about energy not lethargy. Nimble of foot and mind. Adaptable, strong, flexible. That is why we need to see prime ministers and presidents jogging: the message is that they are young and healthy enough to withstand the pressure.

Fourth, the image must be of **understanding business and people problems**. This is about being insightful and supportive. We support our staff, who support our customers, who support us. We care. But we do "tough love." We know what is going on in both the hearts and minds of people.

Never underestimate the power of a good speech or interview – or, indeed, a bad one. For some, like Anita Roddick from The Body Shop appearing on television, it was said to lead to the sudden and dramatic **drop** in the share-price. She came across as scatty.

To give others confidence, you need to be out there talking … to the media, on the shop floor, at brown-bag lunch meetings. But oratory is an art. You need to know the P-words: Pitch, Poetry, Pause and Pace; and the C words: Confidence, Cadence, Conviction, Color. This takes skill, practice and talent.

It is not by chance that so many have learnt their skills in, and through, religious institutions. You need to be able to put over abstract concepts. You need to deal with "doubting Thomases." You need to help those on your side "keep the faith."

The uplifting speech is a performance, and the performer needs to be inebriated with zeal and exuberance. Speech-making is pure theatre. The orator has to be at once proud and humble, powerful and powerless. The speed needs to be both visceral and intellectual. Most of all, it needs to be personal and emotional, exclamatory and climactic.

What are speeches for? To inspire action. But also to feel good about the leader, the cause and, yes, oneself. Speeches are about articulating dreams. They are not full of numbers but, rather, of passionate conviction. Leaders need to be "one of us" to all their listeners. They must really understand inclusivity.

Oratory is, of course, poetry. The writer must understand alliteration and imagery. It is important to use and understand symbolism and meter. No wonder so many great speech-givers are classically trained. And lovers of poetry. The best are spell-binding, mesmeric, hypnotic. They know how to touch the heart: the power of words and phrases. Great speeches are about journeys. No wonder that is the title of Mr Blair's autobiography. Great speeches need to capture a sense of destiny and destination. They create tension by specifying a challenging problem *but*, then, they offer a solution. They must inspire trust: in oneself; one's mission; one's leader.

Business people are re-discovering the power and purpose of narrative. We know that we communicate via stories. So, how to give an inspiring speech. Some suggestions:

- The *first* is the metaphor of the **journey**, or even the **race**. It is about having goals and the journey to reaching them.
- *Second,* speeches must be about **fortitude, tenacity** and **endurance** in the face of setback. Think of Churchill's "the finest hour" speech.
- A *third* theme should be the **fall of the proud**: how cockiness and egotism leads to failure. But hard work, dedication and Stakanovite labor wins in the end.
- *Fourth,* it's quite acceptable if **parents** and **friends** should appear in the talk. They make one human and remind one for whom one is working.

- *Fifth*, the talk must emphasize that we **make our destiny** and our fate. We are the captains of our ship and masters of our fate. Our health, wealth and welfare are in our hands.
- *Sixth*, at the heart of everything is the C-word uttered so often in business settings: **CHANGE**. But better, **PROGRESS**. No surprise that one of the most successfully inspirational books of all time was called *Pilgrim's Progress*.

13 Conspiracy at work

Over 90 percent of employee's think that their bosses know important things about the future of their job that they have not, and will not, talk about. Some believe that their emails are read and their presence recorded on camera. Some believe that members on the board work for the CIA and/or MI5. Some are paranoid; others are, indeed, right.

Who believes in conspiracies at work? Why do some people enjoy "conspiracy ideation," which is the belief in a vast, insidious, preternaturally effective network perpetrating fiendishly complicated and devilishly wicked acts? Some people take easily to conspiracy theories, many of which are well-known, from the assignation of Robert Kennedy, to walking on the moon.

Early work in the area argued that conspiracy theories offered a voice to those who felt powerless or disadvantaged, particularly in the face of crisis when mainstream accounts contained erroneous or unreliable information. A conspiracy theory was seen to provide a convenient alternative to "living with uncertainty." Equally, conspiracist ideation could be seen as a logical response that arises because individuals have little access to accurate information.

But maybe conspiracy theories arise because of an inability to attain specific goals or because they afford a means of maintenance of self-esteem, coping with persecution, reasserting individualism, or expressing negative feelings.

On the other hand, holding conspiracy theories could be a manifestation of the fundamental attribution bias: because of the general tendency to overestimate the importance of dispositional factors and underestimate situational factors. Conspiracy theorists are more likely to blame conspiratorial agents even when there are adequate situational explanations of events. This bias may be heightened when individuals experience intense emotions triggered by catastrophic events, which, in turn, aid the dissemination of conspiracy theories that provide a justification for those emotions.

Conspiracy theories are a manifestation of biased acceptance of information and polarization of attitude. That is, individuals tend to accept, without critique, evidence that is supportive of their own argument, whilst discrediting contrary evidence. But, when people are presented with mixed evidence, they tend to polarize their attitudes, with greater acceptance of their original viewpoint, rather than a reversal of their beliefs. Recent studies show that conspiracy theorists judge fictitious accounts of an assassination to be more plausible if they are consistent with their beliefs, which is called "confirmation bias."

Conspiracy beliefs form part of what is called a "monological belief system," in which a conspiratorial idea serves as evidence for other conspiracist ideation. Thus, for example, people who more strongly endorsed conspiracy theories about the September 11, 2001 (9/11) terrorist attacks were more likely to believe in other, unrelated, conspiracy theories. These monological belief systems afford believers accessible explanations for new phenomena that are difficult to explain or that threaten existing belief systems they have an appetite for.

Researchers have also shown significant associations between conspiracist ideation beliefs and greater anomie/alienation, distrust in authority, political cynicism, powerlessness and lower self-esteem. Conspiracy theorists are not happy people. They feel cynical, marginalized, out-of-the-loop. Also, conspiracist beliefs are associated with a higher authoritarian tendency; they are black/white thinkers.

One recent study by myself and colleagues examined the individual difference correlates of 9/11 conspiracy theories among a representative sample of British respondents (Swami *et al.*, 2010). We found that belief in 9/11 conspiracy theories was strongly associated with belief in other conspiracy theories and exposure (either directly or vicariously) to 9/11 conspiracist ideation. In addition, as predicted, we found significant associations between 9/11 conspiracist ideation and more negative attitudes toward authority, higher political cynicism and greater support for democratic principles. There were some links to personality showing conspiracists to be tough-minded and rather hard-hearted. In short, disagreeable.

Conspiracy or cover-up? The web has spread the word of conspiracy theorists who thrive in dark corners. Of course, governments and business leaders are eager to cover up, paper over and "spin" certain events. Sometimes they succeed, and sometimes not. But beware the colleague whose theories of conspiracy and cover-up extend to behaviors in the organization and beyond.

14 Dark triads and toxic triangles

You don't have to be a numerologist to know of the power of three. All great orators know of the rhythm and the effect of the triple. We rejoice in 3D images, but struggle to be co-operatively coordinated in three-legged races. Politicians respond to the three-line whip. Most national flags seem to have three colours. Bureaucrats want everything in triplicate. Triplanes give extra maneuverability and tripods extra stability. Mysteries come in threes, such as the Holy Trinity. Psychoanalysts have noticed that sexual reproductive organs come in threes. Pornography often portrays wicked threesomes.

And now those interested in bad, sad and mad managers have used the triad and triangle for metaphors, models and mind-maps. The helpless, hopeless and hapless manager is the result of three forces. The trials, tribulations and torments of derailed managers are, it seems, the result.

The dark triad is about people. The toxic triangle about process. To be technical, the dark triad is an intersecting set of three personality characteristics. Machiavellianism, sub-clinical narcissism and sub-clinical psychopathy. People with this profile can show any or all of three related characteristics: cold, manipulative and cynical; a keen sense of entitlement and an unquenchable yearning for admiration, accolades and attention; as well as impulsivity, thrill-seeking and lack of empathy.

Together, the dark triad yield a manager who is self-aggrandizing and aggressive; egocentric and duplicitous, exploitative and callous.

The paradox is that just as many boardrooms as prison cells are occupied by members of the dark triad. Why? If they are bright (and well-educated) as well as good-looking, these dark forces together make for highly proactive, dominant and bold managers. Superficially charming, confident and tough, they are easily noticed. And, if they move quickly, their hit-and-run, selfish, short-termism means they are unlikely to be found out.

They are amoral rather than immoral, "a-loyal" rather than disloyal. And they can be very successful in certain business situations. Amidst the fast-moving, the unstable, the threatening, they do well. The empathic, self-effacing, law abiding managers bite the dust.

Hence the paradox and the irony. Dark triad managers often do well … for a time. But there is a God. Most self destruct and get their come-uppance. Fortunately, on their own they can often do little damage. Why? The answer lies in the toxic triangle. It is not enough to be a destructive, derailing or a deranged leader to do damage. That makes up only part of the triangle.

The other two factors are the susceptibility of the followers and the conduciveness of the environment. First, the followers. Could Hitler have led the British, or Mussolini the Germans? The Brits don't respond well to Fascists, as Oswald Mosley found. We find them faintly ridiculous, laughable rather than laudable, and have a strong desire to puncture their pomposity.

Some groups are more gullible than others: those humiliated by defeat; those honed by ideology; those scared of the unknown. Clever leaders tell people what they want to hear. Hence the contrast of the "I have nothing to offer but blood, toil, tears and sweat" of Churchill to the "Deutschland uber alles" invective of old Adolf. Leaders, good and bad, need the support of followers at most stages of their career, particularly at the beginning.

Followers can be driven by greed as well as fear in great promises of wealth, fame and power; and influenced by rhetoric itself.

But a destructive leader and a group of susceptible followers still isn't enough. One needs a conducive environment. In business, this means one lightly or not-at-all regulated. Or it may be in a time of great change or invention with new products or services. Companies put in place many processes and procedures, checks and balances to guard against the excesses of megalomania from incautious or deluded CEOs. They temper their discretion.

The places where bad, immoral leaders most thrive are in unregulated, emergent markets, or in countries that have little history of democratic institutions. Equally, times of crisis – such as terrorism, currency collapse, or rapid change – mean that rule-following is ignored or forgotten.

The idea is simple. If you are unlucky enough to have someone with the dark triad of traits running a company of naïve followers in a poorly-regulated environment, you get pure, unalloyed toxicity.

Everyone who has watched children's television or tried for the fire-fighter's badge knows you only get combustion and fire if there is heat, fuel and oxygen. The heat of the manager, the fuel of the followers and the oxygen of discretion.

Perhaps that is why hazard warning signs themselves are triangles.

15 Dealing with opponents

Orthodoxy in business is rarer than in politics and religion, but no less interesting. The idea that there is one – and only one – efficient, good and proper way to do things can be found in accountants, engineers and IT people. It can even be found in management.

Whilst management fads, fortunately perhaps, don't last too long, they do encourage consultant-led believers. So, there were the process re-engineering puritans; the balanced score card believers and the empowerment evangelists.

Organizations like alignment, and true believers can have enough power and influence to force underlings to tow the party line and, at least superficially, behaviorally "play the game."

But what does history teach us about attempts to convert to the one true faith of anything. First, the more one has orthodoxy, the more clear it becomes who are heretics. Rules, regulations and behavioral requirements soon show who is with one and who is against one. One can only be a heretic if there is a rigid orthodoxy.

Action and reaction. Indeed, the Freudians call it reaction-formation. The idea is that a mirror image of an ideology or system occurs. The Church of England does not have (many) heretics, but Islam does.

Orthodoxy leads to the emergence of heretics. And what follows is their persecution. This, of course, strengthens their beliefs. Ignore, laugh at or disregard odd heretics and they wither away. Concentrate your fire on them and you give them the oxygen of publicity.

The boomerang effect of banning is very well-known. Ban a book, a film and a speaker and you act as an excellent advertisement. Sales go up. Paradoxically, some people strive to have their product banned or critiqued by the establishment: they know it can do them no end of good with young people, liberals or outsiders.

Advertisers also know this. Put in an age restriction, and it really encourages the under-aged. Ban a pamphlet, and presses have to roll overtime to print enough to satiate the curiosity of others. Stop people parading, marking and speaking, and you only attract attention to their cause.

The final act is targeting individuals by fining them, imprisoning them or, worse, killing them. Martyrdom is by far the best recruiting sergeant. We had the metric martyrs who set back the metric campaign by years. We have the council tax martyrs: all persecuted by law.

By-and-large, the English deal well with deviants. Where else would you find Hyde Park Corner: a place dedicated to the ravings of the unorthodox. The BBC have always dealt with young iconoclasts well. You give them a series on the television.

The politically correct obsessionals do things in a very non-English way. The words, "nigger," "gollywog," and so on have, largely, faded from everyday speech. Punish – rather than lampoon – speakers of the words, and you get a terrible backlash against all controlled speech.

So, what has all this got to do with business? It's got most to do with zealotry. People in the business of change do zero tolerance. You get zero tolerance from accounts and HR and health-and-safety. There is one prescribed, correct, orthodox way. There is the way, the truth and the light. And woe betide you, if you stray.

The change agent is faced always by resistance. He or she may adopt a wide range of strategies to persuade people to change long-held and clear attitudes and behaviors. They may try bribery (sorry … monetary incentives) or re-engineering. Some get political, targeting particular stakeholders; others go for meetings and seminars to talk about issues.

But whatever you do, if there is a firm bunch of resistors, snipe at every opportunity.

16   Defending the self

Ever seen a CEO in distress? Of course. What is really interesting is how they cope. We do many things when stressed: phone a friend or pour a stiff G&T; go for a jog or pray; have a nap or go to bed. Some are healthier than others; some work better than others. And, over time, we tend to develop a preferred coping strategy, a subject that fascinated Anna Freud, daughter of the great Sigmund.

According to orthodox, Freudian, psychoanalytic theory, defense mechanisms are the psychological strategies people use unconsciously to cope with reality and stresses that occur in everyday working life. They are used by healthy persons throughout life and only become pathological when constantly over-used, generating abnormal behavior where the physical or psychological health of the individual is affected severely. They are, essentially, a coping device.

These defense mechanisms have been categorized from "healthy" to "unhealthy." At the bottom of the pile, *Level 1*, are four easily recognizable and somewhat ineffective strategies: delusions, denial, distortion and splitting.

Delusions: extreme delusions about external reality; often a false belief that others are conspiring to harm that individual (sometimes known as "persecutory delusion"). For politicians, it is the media; for CEOs, perhaps shareholders or city bankers.

Denial: a refusal to accept an external situation because one finds it too threatening; to deny the existence of any provoking situation(s); reducing one's own anxiety level by not acknowledging unpleasant aspects of external reality. "Crisis, what crisis?"

Distortion: changing and reshaping reality as one sees fit; seeking only information that confirms one's view of the world.

Splitting: a primitive mechanism whereby negative and positive impulses are split and not integrated with each other. The individual is two people … the good guy refusing to accept the bad guy. Not Jekyll and Hyde or schizophrenia: that is a very serious illness.

The mechanisms at *Level 2* are commonly found in adolescents, because people who use these defense mechanisms in excess are often seen as immature and socially undesirable. These defenses include acting out, fantasy, idealization, passive aggression, projection and somatization:

Acting out: an unconscious expression or impulse without being aware of the emotion behind it (watch the X factor to understand this).

Fantasy: the tendency to escape reality to resolve internal and external conflicts; this may include imagining revenge or your own death, or excessive day dreaming; belief that you alone are responsible for a hike in the share price, or that all your staff really admire you.

Idealization: perceiving other individuals to possess more positive qualities than they actually have; refusing to see the negative flaws in others. This is rare at work but common in the classroom and playground.

Passive aggression: expressing anger or frustration, through indirect methods, about other people. This is very common: the sniping, sour, whistle-blowing type of executive who feels perpetually hard done by.

Projection: a primitive form of paranoia that supposedly lessens anxiety by shifting undesirable thoughts, feelings and impulses on to someone else. They become bad objects: repositories of everything bad. This is a deep urge to see all that one hates in oneself in others: gluttonous, greedy, deprivation.

Somatization: now common, this is when negative feelings towards other people are directed on to the self and one becomes ill. There is a whole range of "preferred," even acceptable, psychosomatic illnesses nowadays. The stress headache, sensitive stomach, skin rash are well-known examples.

Level 3 defenses are considered neurotic. They have short-term benefits in coping, but may cause problems in relationships, work and overall satisfaction of life, if used as the predominant way of coping. These defenses include displacement, dissociation, hypochrondriasis, intellectualization, isolation, rationalization, reaction formation, regression, repression and undoing.

Displacement: shifting emotions onto another target (that may be more acceptable or less threatening).

Dissociation: an extreme change of one's personal identity to avoid emotional distress for a short period of time; separating or postponing a feeling attributed to a particular situation.

Hypochrondriasis: perceiving to have an unknown illness as a reaction to negative feelings toward others.

Intellectualization: using logic and intellectual components of a situation to distance oneself.

Isolation: separating emotions from events; talking about a situation without displaying any feelings about it.

Rationalization: convincing oneself that things are fine through false rationality; "making excuses" for a situational outcome.

Reaction formation: reversing emotions; behaving in a manner that is the opposite of how one truly feels; taking an opposite belief, since the true belief will cause anxiety.

Regression: reverting to an earlier stage of development rather than handling the unpleasant situation in a more adult way.

Repression: preventing uncomfortable thoughts entering the conscious.

Undoing: trying to "undo" an unhealthy, destructive or threatening thought by acting contrarily.

At the top of the tree, *Level 4*, are mature defense mechanisms present in emotionally healthy adults. These defenses have been adapted over time in order to cope with life. They help eliminate the conflicting emotions and thoughts that arise under stress. These defenses include anticipation, humor, identification, introjection, sublimation and thought suppression.

Anticipation: knowing and accepting that future discomfort may occur and trying to be better prepared.

Humor: expressing unpleasant thoughts in a humorous way; making fun of uncomfortable situations; putting things in proportion by seeing the ludicrous side of things.

Identification: unconscious modeling of another person's character or behavior.

Introjection: identifying with an idea or object so much that it becomes part of oneself.

Sublimation: Turning negative emotions into more positive actions, behavior or emotions.

Thought suppression: consciously pushing thoughts into the unconscious; not paying attention to an emotion in order to cope with the present situation.

So? Tick any boxes for yourself and others? Are you still partly stuck at primitive Level 1, or working your Level 4 healthy defenses well? Being able to employ more of the healthy defenses is clearly beneficial. What is "your poison," in the sense of a preferred group of defense mechanisms? Can they ever be changed? Yes … but it may take time, effort, money and painful therapy.

17 The disaffected worker

We all recognize them in the workplace: the passed over and pissed-off; those in the departure lounge; the bitter, passive-aggressive, "*nyet*-oriented" types. The individual who astutely removes both brain and heart before crossing the threshold of work.

Sour, miserable and poisonous. They often command all the energy of managers for little or no reward. They are the alienated: not only from the products of their labor, but also management, the company as a whole and certainly their engaged colleagues.

Are they more common in the public than the private sector? Are they mostly of a "certain age?" The two questions that exercise people most about the alienated worker are, *first*, "Why are they/did they become like that?" and, *second*, "How do we cure/solve the problem?" The first question not only informs the second, but also gives warnings about how to prevent these problem cases arising.

Most people don't begin their working lives alienated, disaffected and disenchanted. Something happens to them, sometimes quite early in their lives. This can scar and wound them. Some never recover: others are strengthened and made more resilient as a function of the experience.

There are around five common causes:

The personality of the worker: we have known for years now that job satisfaction is partly heritable. The unstable, moody introvert is prone to negativism, melancholia and generalized unhappiness They are gloom carriers: always stressed, always miserable, always feeling badly dealt with. They are naturals for disaffection.

Getting in with a bad lot: work groups shape beliefs and behaviors. They can turn eager, enthusiastic young people into militant clock-watchers. They can inculcate bad attitudes and values that stay with an individual long after these groups have broken up.

The experience of bad managers: there is nothing like a cold bully or a two-faced psychopathic boss to "turn a person." Weak managers who won't confront poor performance are as likely to cause disaffection as indifferent managers who care only about their personal career.

Poor management systems: if a person has been badly managed it may be because there is no system in place. Their expectations are not managed, they do not have progress reviews, appraisals are a loathed and pointless paper-chase. The managers have no management skills and techniques, and there are no processes that encourage good management.

Facing change: the "C" word causes both boredom (talk about change all the time) and anxiety (it is difficult and uncomfortable). There are changes in technology, customer expectations and competition. What if one works for a company in decline, or that makes a product or produces a service no longer required. "Adapt or die" is hard to hear. Dig in, resist and strike seem to some the only alternative to learning new skills and starting over.

But the question most managers ask is: "What to do? How to solve this problem?" They all recognize the type. They all know, to their cost, how much energy they waste on these characters, and how difficult they can be. Most would, if they could, simply sack them at the first opportunity. They believe these individuals are, for the most part irredeemable. There are four things that can be done: physically move people, restructure, take performance management seriously, and assessment/development centers.

Physically move people: the alienated form clubs and cabals. They sit in the same seat in the cafeteria every day. They can be militant. And because they form these groups, they think that others are like them and that their beliefs and behaviors are normal. So, break them up by moving them physically. Surround them by young enthusiastic people. Unfreeze their comfort zone. Rearrange the furniture. Use any opportunity to change their surroundings. Remember: the single-most powerful predictor of who makes friends with whom at work is propinquity or proximity. Start by breaking up groups.

Restructure: perhaps the easiest method. Don't try voluntary severance: that never gets rid of them. It only encourages the talented to move. Fiddle with the chart seriously every three years. You might even form a subsidiary with all the alienated together in one group: and then sell it at a bargain price to a venture capitalist.

Take performance management seriously: you can teach an old dog new tricks – but it takes effort. The first step in privatization is often performance management. Individuals are rewarded and remunerated not for length of service but, rather, for performance. People need clear, relevant and stretching goals that should be measurable. They need help and support in attaining those goals, and feedback on how they are doing. They need their expectations managed, and they need to see a clear relationship between all aspects of their (and others') work performance and rewards. Equitable, fair and open.

Assessment/development centers: perhaps people need an MOT or check-up every so often – like cars; or like pilots who have, by law, to subject themselves to a careful, thorough and subtle audit by an **outside person/ body** who is there to be more objective. The disenchanted and disaffected don't believe anything management tells them, but they may listen to an outsider.

There will always be the discontented and disenchanted; those resent-ful and rebellious towards authority. Some are inherently like that; most are the result of poor management. And, of course, prevention is better than cure.

18 Divergent thinking

Would you prefer your CEO to be an arts or science graduate? Does it matter? What if they had a first degree in French or history or philosophy, as opposed to mathematics or physics or zoology? What about media studies or sociology or women's studies? And what if they had higher degrees in these subjects, indicating a real passion? Or perhaps an attempt to defer adulthood and getting a job.

Most would probably argue that, as long as any potential CEO has an MBA and/or good experience *and* a good record, it does not really matter. If they are bright, hard-working and dedicated, that is enough. But do arts and science graduates think differently? Have they very different skills and preferences?

There has long been an interest in the different thinking styles of those in the arts and those in science. This debate was structured by C.P. Snow in his 1959 lecture entitled *The Two Cultures*. He stressed the differences and poor communication between the sciences and the humanities.

It was the work of Liam Hudson in the sixties that stimulated psychological research in this area. He wrote a wonderful book called *Contrary Imaginations* (1967) that argued that a person's personality counts for as much as ability in their choice of, and academic success in, different subjects.

He studied English schoolboys, and found that conventional measures of intelligence used at the time did not always do justice to their abilities. The tests gave credit for problem-solving that produced the "right" answer, but underestimated creativity and unconventional approaches to problems.

He concluded that there were two different forms of thinking or ability: "convergent" thinking and "divergent" thinking. Convergent thinking applies where the person is good at bringing material from a variety of sources to bear on a problem in such a way as to produce the "correct" answer. This kind of thinking is particularly appropriate in science and math, and also facilitates good scores on intelligence tests.

Divergent thinking is characterized by a broad creative elaboration of ideas prompted by some stimulus, and is more suited to artistic pursuits and study of the humanities.

It seemed, then, that conventional approaches to assessment might be seriously underestimating the talent of a section of the school population. It also suggests that the way children are taught seems only to benefit convergent thinkers.

There are many tests of divergent thinking. Try the following:

> In two minutes (only), write down as *quickly as possible* and as *many as possible*, and as *unusual as possible*, things you could do with a ... paper clip (or hot water bottle, wooden barrel). How many did you get? Some people get well over 20. And how many are verging on the disgusting: pick your nose/ears/ teeth, stab an insect, create a tattoo?
>
> In five minutes, write down all the possible major and minor consequences if we never had to eat again (or if everyone went blind). Again, count them up, and look for evidence of really unusual ones.

You soon notice serious and significant differences between people. Some really enjoy the exercise. They seem cognitively disinhibited. They happily come up with many and strange ideas. Others find the process neither fun nor natural.

Another example is manifest in traditional **brainstorming**, now called "thought-showering" by the politically correct. By "piggy-backing" on the suggestions of others and no criticism allowed for "daft, impractical" ideas, the hope is that you open wide your mind and let your imagination run wild. Clearly, some people really enjoy the whole brainstorming experience and enter into the fun and games approach. Marketing types perhaps?

As one may expect, divergent thinking is thought of as a measure of creativity. So, does this come down to anything more than asking if "arty-farty" creative types are wanted, or needed, to head up the organization. Most people would say, very emphatically, NO. None of all of that impractical, unpredictable, off-the-wall stuff, thank you. Give me, any day, the competent, focused problem-solver.

But is this a fair dichotomy? This is not an either/or; it can be a both/and. Thinking styles show preferences. Divergent, like extrovert, at one end; convergent like introvert, at the other. Most of us are in-between. There are often disadvantages with being at extremes; though, with special talents, it can signal many advantages as well.

Business is about problem-finding **and** solving; it is about coming up with novel ideas and products, and testing them. Look at the *Dragons' Den*. It is often a case of creative, divergent thinkers seeking help from an experienced convergent dragon who tumbles the numbers.

Those silos we hear about contain people with similar styles: so yes, marketing has more divergent thinkers and finance more convergent thinkers. That is why the concept of "creative accountancy" is so amusing; a bit like "scientific marketing."

Strongly divergent and convergent thinkers can bring a great deal to business. Coupled with intelligence and hard work, either of these thinking styles can lead to great success but, as in all things, moderation often wins out. Or, of course, a group with people from either extreme … though they are hardly likely to get on with one another!

19 Does coaching work?

It is easy to be skeptical – indeed, cynical – about executive coaches. The sacked, sour and screwed-up executive one day: the executive coach the next. But this is clearly more than a fad or fashion that disappears by the end of the fiscal year. It is a massive growth industry, even if supply seems to have exceeded demand.

The growth in mental health professions over the last 25 years in most developed countries has been spectacular. And those paying for these services have also been clamoring to rationalize the expense by showing that treatment really is effective. What, they ask, is the active ingredient? If, of course, there is one.

Academics have tried to provide both an answer and a percentage; that is, how important each explanatory factor is. Interestingly the four factors apply (roughly) equally to all forms of counseling, therapy, coaching, or whatever the help is called.

Ingredient 1: **client factors**. It is, in short, more important to know *who* (what kind of person) has the problem than *what* the problem is. This accounts for a whopping **40 percent** of the effect. It is accurately reflected in the old joke "How many psychologists does it take to change a light bulb? Answer: only one. But the light bulb needs to want to be changed."

It's called **readiness for coaching**. It is a mixture of being willing and able to learn, to change, to embrace challenge. The coach needs to assess and then stimulate readiness; remove barriers and resistance to moving on. Further, the professional needs to respond to clients' preferences. Some (they are called "internalizers") want insight; others (called "externalizers") want symptom-focused approaches. Much depends on whether the client is a conscript or a volunteer; if the latter, what they think they are signing up for. This is why there is a first meeting, prior to the "sign up."

There is a bit of a paradox here. If 40 percent of the success of coaching comes from client dispositions, then coaches can, at most, take only 60 percent of the credit for the magic they perform. So, it's dangerous for the coach to develop hubris. Some clients are eminently coachable (however much you do) and others are not. Often, those who need it most resist it most, and *vice versa*.

Ingredient 2: "It's the **relationship**, stupid." The coach can explore and exploit the therapeutic alliance. It's about collaboration, consensus and support. It's the effective and affective bond. Again, this has to be tailored to the client. It is about building and maintaining a positive, open, productive and, hopefully, transformative alliance.

However, it should be pointed out that it is the client and not the coach's explanation of the alliance that is important: coaches need to check this fact with their clients regularly. The distracted, fatigued or unprepared coach is a poor coach. The alliance is usually based on set and agreed goals and tasks.

Ingredient 3, which buys you 15 percent of the result, is that old-fashioned quality sometimes called "hope," and now called **expectations**. It is about expectation of improvement, finding new paths to goals and "agency thinking:" the belief that one can, if one tries.

Coaches speak and leak the message that successful change or progress is possible. They actuate hope by building credibility at the beginning of the relationship. Clients can detect loss of faith in the project by the coach.

And Ingredient 4 is the application of every/**any theory and therapy**. It accounts for 15 percent of the power of coaching. The use of healing rites and rituals. The coaches' backgrounds influence their focus. Whilst some look at organizational competition, conflict, dominance and power, others may look at self-awareness and encourage personal SWOTS: the standard old strengths, weaknesses, opportunities, threats.

Theories organize observation. Some coaches share them with their clients, others don't. Clearly, the good coach needs to know what works for whom. But coaches also need to know about the business world and the dilemma of conflict of interests between the client and the organization. Coaches really have to be business savvy. They need to read the *FT* not Freud; the *Economist*, not Erikson.

The client–coach mission and relationship is a bit like that of the patient–therapist. But there are differences. Typically, patients have more serious problems and poorer adjustment than business clients. Therapists work at a deeper emotional level than a coach. Therapists see more of the patient, and contact is nearly always face-to-face. Coaches focus on the workplace; therapists work on all aspects of functioning.

Patients often seek personal growth and alleviation of suffering; coaching clients, enhanced work performance. Coaching clients seek to enhance their emotional intelligence, political prowess and their understanding of cultural differences.

So, there we have it. Coaching only works if the client is able, ready and willing. It works well if the bond is good. And if the coach instills hope for change. Would an internal mentor do as well? Perhaps. But the external, unbiased objectivity of an outside coach is often very preferable

Are some executives un-coachable? Clearly. Is coaching worth the money? Sometimes.

20 Dysfunctional credentialism

What do you do or say when an old (bald as a coot) friend suddenly pitches up in a wig? The follicly challenged are quite naturally tempted to "recapture" their youthfulness, good looks and "pull-ability" by investing often-extensive sums in a wig or hair piece. Do you pretend not to notice; comment on their fitness; or tease them gently or even unmercifully for their vanity or stupidity? A matter of taste, an indicator of friendship or a function of your emotional intelligence? What precisely is good form?

And what about another, perhaps less common but odder scenario. An old friend with just OK school results pitches up one day with a BSc, an MBA and a PhD after his name. For years, he had been accumulating, rather desperately, odd sets of letters, industry membership or fellowship of strange, self-important and semi-bogus organizations. Now he has the full set – 10 years of education at the stroke of a brush: read "very large check to a greedy organization that gives you degrees for life experience."

Is this different from a graying middle-manager with few qualifications suddenly being introduced as Professor Smith? He got an "honorary, special, visiting … " or some other Professorship from the University of Southern North Dakota in exchange for a few lectures to MBAs. A good deal for both; or a case of deception?

There are two issues here: titular yearnings and bogus credentialism. Like the wig, they are disguises. But are they dangerous, immoral or wrong? Or is it an indication of being pathetic rather than devious. The answer to the question lies in such things as the motives for the change but, more, it depends on the effect on the person rather than his or her customers, friends or peers.

What if the wig-wearer becomes unable to play sports because of fearing the wig might fall off? What if they will never again appear wigless, for fear of humiliation? But what if their wig-wearing turns them into a mid-life Lothario? What if they become suddenly empowered to being almost a sexual predator with their new found crown of glory?

In business, credentials are sometimes very important. Often, you need to be a licensed, chartered member of some society or body (like the BMA or the BPS) to practice. You have to have had the training to acquire the knowledge and skills to "do the business:" flying a plane, undertaking a brain surgery, seeing a patient. Most of us want that – we need to know that people are properly trained by recognized authorities to do their job. But where does this process begin and end? What about "foreign training?" And training to what standard? Does the training institution matter? Does experience "trump" training? Should certificates have an expiry date?

The problems are particularly apparent in business: in general management, but also in coaching and training. Does the fact that a manager has an MBA make him or her a better manager? Should your business coach be able to boast some accredited training course? Do you need a post-graduate degree to be a competent or superior technical trainer?

There seems no doubt that qualifications make a difference. Indeed, many managers soon work out the value of an MBA. The story goes like this: MBAs are seriously expensive – particularly if you calculate opportunity costs, as well as costs to one's private life. Let's say $150K. How long does it take to recoup that investment? Does it ensure or at least "considerably facilitate" a quick rise in salary?

Some lecturers say how extrinsically motivated MBA and other business degree students are. They really want that piece of paper – those magical letters. It is a deal, but also a bet. It has magical career accelerating powers. So, they do what is required … and no more. Others ask how one could ever become a seriously competent senior manager without the knowledge of finance, marketing and business processes that the degree offers. The answer to that is to look at the sheer number of entrepreneurs who never went to university, let alone received an MBA.

All of us want our professionals trained and qualified to do the job. Certainly, we want our pilots and our surgeons well trained. We also want our teachers and nurses trained. And our hairdressers.

But what of those in any profession who make too much of these qualifications? Why it is that coaches, trainers and business book writers make so much of their qualifications, for which many pay large amounts of money?

21 Elite performers

Most of us would love to be thought as elite performers; top-of-the-class, really talented. They surely are most sought-after at work. The simply gifted: those who, apparently effortlessly, bring home the golden prizes. Top of the tree ... and all that.

To be an elite anything takes masses of effort, training and determination. It's often easier to describe an elite performer than to understand how they became so good. They seem to see patterns differently and read situations faster, they seem to have a bigger repertoire of options, they seem more confident and in control. It all looks so effortless; but that is very definitely not the case. (See Malcolm Gladwell's many books on this particular subject.)

Studies of elite performers in the arts, sports and sciences have thrown up some really interesting findings. *First*, there is the 10-year rule. As a rule of thumb, it takes 10 years of intensive, focused "full-on" training and practice to get you there as an elite performer. That is a decade: that is dedication. Study the lives of top athletes, academics and musicians and you will see how true that is. Nothing comes without effort, and this is serious effort.

Second, elite performers seem to know how to maximize practice. This means they may do as little as four or five hours per day, but they break this into no more than hour-long sessions, and they often have little naps between them. It's what the creativity researchers call "incubation." Work hard, but rest: let it all seep in. Learn how to learn.

Third, these people challenge themselves. They make it difficult for themselves. They prefer not to automate responses. They try out new ways of doing things. As a result, in practice – but in practice only – they often look less skilled and polished than less-talented performers. They experiment; and they set themselves tough, but attainable targets. Note: they set them – not their coach or colleagues – they themselves.

Thus, by these calculations, to see the performance for 30 minutes to an hour of an elite athlete or musician takes the 20,000 hours of practice. That is a serious investment. That is the real commitment involved to be at the top of one's game.

How, and for how long, people practice a skill and knowledge acquisition is crucial. One has to *invest* – seriously invest – time and expertise for the sake of one's art or sport or discipline. And this inevitably involves eschewing other, often very attractive, activities. In this sense some, but by no means all, elite performers seem a little narrow: even a little naïve. When others went partying, on holiday, to leisure events, the aspirant elites practiced. They have to have iron discipline and a very real desire to "win" to get there.

And most know, there is a window in their lives where things are possible. It may have to do with physical fitness, energy or even financial constraints. Life, they know, is not a dress rehearsal.

But is that all? What about talent, abilities and genes? Training *unlocks* the genes; practice helps biology become destiny. Many people with prodigious talent seem to ignore it, down-play it or simply fail to exploit it. They happily adopt that oh-so-British policy of self-deprecation that both disarms and perplexes foreigners. Further, this is also never understood by many contestants on those ubiquitous talent shows.

The training required to be an elite performer in any field is exceptionally demanding. It looks all very easy. It is patently not.

So, elite performers need a good start in life in two ways: their genetics and their parents (who give guidance and support, provide opportunities – indeed, help them find their talents), which are closely linked. They also need the sheer drive to succeed. This drive is their investment to do the training. It is the practice that is key. It is how, for how long and to what end that performer's practice really unlocks the genetic endowment and background advantages.

To look at talented and elite performers in any sphere we tend to forget:

- How much they have practiced, and do and will practice.
- What they have sacrificed for the skill.
- How they set their own targets.
- How driven they have had to be.
- How little they believe in chance, luck and personal gifts.

This is clearly not the message that one gets from self-help books or from management books, or from the movies. They make it all rather simple, almost effortless. And that is seriously misleading, as can be found from most honest(ish) autobiographies.

There is also the issue of dealing with setbacks. One has, in any competitive area, to learn how to deal with a range of problems: stage fright, physical injury, being beaten by brilliant opponents. These experiences toughen up the elite performer but break the less well-adjusted. There is nothing like adversity to focus drive and determination.

Students of the magical MBA or the part-time degree know the sacrifice that is involved there. If there are 24 hours in a day of which you sleep one third, how much of the remainder do you give to your friends/family and work?

The mastery of any skill comes easier to the talented, but all skills take practice. This includes all those skills one goes on training courses to achieve: presentational skills, negotiation skills, counseling skills and selling skills.

Remember the riposte to the question: How do you get to the Albert Hall or the Olympic stadium? The answer is not geographical but behavioral: it is "practice, practice, practice."

22   Employ-worthiness

The headlines at times of depression, double-dip and bear markets are all rather depressing. More and more (bright, young, qualified) people chasing fewer and fewer jobs; graduates having to do menial, sometimes even unpaid, work; middle-aged, middle-brow, middle-managers thrown on the dust heap … forever. Pipe and slippers, whether you like it or not.

It is hard to get a job nowadays. 'Twasn't always thus. But most employers have always been "picky." Perhaps they have had clearly articulated selection criteria, perhaps they trust their intuition. But now they are faced with huge numbers of applicants for almost every position. So what to look for … what are the markers of happy, healthy and productive workers?

What does it take to make you employable? This may take rather different skills depending on whether you are interested in what it takes to get a job (hiring), hold a job (retaining) and thrive in a job (promotion). Indeed, the people responsible for hiring may be very different from those who supervise them or those that ensure they get promoted. Indeed, the charm and guile and self-awareness that may help people *get* jobs may, in certain circumstances, handicap them from doing the job well.

The selector is usually faced with piles of CVs: all with those hubris-filled, introductory paragraphs claiming the person is dynamic, conscientious, emotionally literate and so on. And they now have an astonishing array of qualifications. What is a 2/2 in Tourism Studies from the University of the Watford Gap worth? What does it indicate? How about an A* in an A-level called "Modern Technology"?

So, what do most want? Certainly, there may be different criteria depending on sector, level and skills.

There seem to be at least three schools of thought:

Select for attitude (i.e. drive), train skills. This school of thought argues that it is motivation, more than education or qualifications, that one should look for. But motivation is very difficult to assess, partly because people may not have sufficient insight into their own motives. Certainly, the Freudians would concur. But you can certainly get at motivation by looking at past behavior. What evidence is there that the person is a self-starter, a natural entrepreneur, a wise risk-taker? People who are hungry are easy to train. People who are driven only need pointing in the right direction.

Select for ability, socialize the work ethic. This school places great emphasis on ability (read "intelligence") as the key. They know bright people learn faster. They know they make better decisions, understand complex data and tend to be good at strategy. They also argue, correctly, that intelligence is relatively easy to measure accurately. They also know the worth of the work ethic. Conscientiousness, prudence, need for achievement. They assume that can be, in part, trained. Through carrots and sticks and the good common sense that comes with intelligence, they will pick up the real need for the work ethic.

Select for know-how and skills, shape personal style. Employers want people to be able to deliver products and process sometimes very complex information. This can require much training, knowledge and appropriate qualifications. So, they select for what people can do. But they know that is not enough: they need charm, social skills and emotional intelligence, sometimes thought of as being a style. This they hope to "instill."

The question for the selector is what is most trainable and what the least. That which you can change or develop most, you train. And that which may be fairly fused by genes or early upbringing, you select for.

The answer is clear: you can't teach ability and you can't teach drive/attitude: so, this is what you select for.

23　Engagement isn't enough

As all consultants know, you have to re-package and re-label old ideas or concepts to make them more marketable. So, we used to have "job satisfaction," which then became "job involvement," which later changed into "organizational commitment."

But now (fanfare and happy jingle) we have the new-and-improved "job engagement." And boy do you need it, because it cures all known problems: job engagement reduces absenteeism and turnover; it promotes productivity and well-being. It has the new, scientifically proven, magic ingredient: worker motivation. The engaged worker will be the healthy, happy, productive worker, never going absent or on strike, and being contented with their lot.

Job satisfaction seemed pretty important, as it was assumed that satisfied workers were more productive. Therefore, one of the key management tasks was to make people happy. Unfortunately, three pieces of research led to the discrediting of this idea. *First*, happiness was found to be very clearly related to personality, particularly emotional adjustment. Less well-adjusted (more neurotic) people are more dissatisfied with every job they have, however nice their bosses, good their pay, pleasant their working conditions. They are carriers of gloom, dissatisfaction, and general antipathy. And the opposite: stable, extroverts are happy people whatever the circumstances.

Second, there is as much evidence that productivity caused satisfaction as the reverse. This suggests that, if you help people to be more productive, they become happier rather than the other way around. We got the direction of causality wrong. The successful worker is manifoldly rewarded, which makes them happy. *Third*, job satisfaction is an idea and a feeling, and has little to do with motivation. It does not have motivational force: it is only very loosely related to any form of productivity. It is a reaction to circumstance.

So, the pundits talked about being job-involved. People who were involved seemed very focused on their particular task. This was all well and good, but many seemed little interested and concerned with others or the general productivity of the organization. In that sense, it could even be said to be an index of egocentricity. We have all met the involved, somewhat obsessed worker who is happy-ish but ultimately unproductive, caught up in their funny little processes.

For this reason, the words changed to organizational (not just personal) commitment. But this is a concept of the head, not the heart, and does not necessarily explain what the person is committed to or, indeed, why. Workers may be so committed they want to see no change or development in the organization. Commitment can also mean entrapment. After all, you are committed to a mental hospital.

So, how do we describe the individuals who are clearly physically, cognitively and emotionally active at work: the employees who give and get; who are motivated and derive meaning from their job? Engaged … the opposite of which is the worker who is alienated or who "decouples" the self from the work role.

Engaged workers are motivated and happy because the work allows them to explore their talents and values successfully, and offers them meaning and reward. Engaged people have vigor and energy; they are dedicated to their task, company, customers and peers; and they tend to be involved. Where are these wunderkinder? Can I turn my taciturn, "*nyet*"-oriented, gloom-merchant staff into engaged workers?

Are there more or less engage-able people, both bosses and workers? Perhaps some jobs are more engage-worthy than others. Stable and hard-working people are easier to engage. Amen. Some people seem constantly cheery, upbeat and positive. They are the life-enhancers we all seek, as opposed to the negative, soul-destroying, cynical individuals at the other end of the spectrum.

Engage-ability is linked to the personality traits of adjustment (low neuroticism) and conscientiousness (prudence). It is also linked to agree-ableness and altruism. Some people are, thus, easy to engage by head and heart, and others not. This applies to bosses and workers alike. Call it inspiration or charisma, some leaders have it and engage all those around them, and others don't. Unfortunately, training courses don't help much.

Engagement comes partly from employee–manager relationships. If they see where their work fits into the big picture, they are more likely to feel engaged. If they feel fairly dealt with and listened to, they are more likely to feel engaged; as is also the case if they feel valued and valuable. So, engagement is part of the processes and procedures of the organization. That is why HR is interested, but their heavy-handed, prescriptive, bureaucratic approach can easily destroy any hope of real engagement.

So, how easy is it to engage a traffic warden or a street cleaner? Some jobs are tedious, dull and under-skilled. Think of those people in cities who hold up signs pointing the way to stores having sales, or to restaurants. The "job" only exists as a result of some petty by-laws on advertising.

Contrast this with the ability to engage an amateur choir, or a group at work chosen because they are high-flyers. By definition, those who are intrinsically motivated don't need very much extrinsic motivation. We all need encouragement and feedback and support.

Engagement chimes with that other fashionable concept: emotional intelligence. Indeed, what they have in common is the recognition of the power of affect of emotion. We are socio-emotional animals. We live in groups. We need to belong, to help others and be supported. These are emotional issues, and the job satisfaction researchers have at last picked this up.

24 The entrepreneurial spirit

It is very difficult indeed to get into the top consultancy firms these days: but then, it always was. Bright-eyed, multi-lingual, MBA after "An A-starred-first-class degree," young people fight hard to join the ranks of mostly American-owned and based consultancies.

Many now seek out the sexier world of traditional management consultancy, as banking and private equity and hedge funds have lost their glamour a little, but not entirely!

Potential management consultants seek the excitement, the glamour and the money. It is an addictive, work-hard–play-hard lifestyle that can mesmerize and beguile. Consultants (and bankers) are in the fast stream and the slipstream: the white water rafters of business. Still glamorous after all these years.

Consultancy firms know what they are looking for. They know the model that works. Many recruit in Great Britain only from the golden-triangle universities (Oxbridge and London). They know that students there are smart and well-socialized. They also show preferences for certain business schools. Consultancy businesses know that their staff need to be fit and resilient. They work long hours with difficult material and difficult clients. They need to be "presentable" and have considerable social skills to impress clients twice their age. They need to be persuasive and quick-witted.

Of course, they need to understand how business works. They might not be in possession of that extremely important MBA certificate, but they certainly should be able to comprehend the basic functions of business. Clever students can pick this up. The historian or the classicist can do just as well as the mathematician or economics graduate.

They need EQ and IQ (emotional and cognitive intelligence). They need to be grown-up and responsible. They need to be able to charm and persuade CEOs twice their age and from the hard-knocks school.

But they need something more: entrepreneurial spirit. A taste for enterprise. Years ago, one consultancy believed this was a crucial indicator of consultant talent. Applicants may have had all sorts of worthy CV-fodder activities, from President of the Union to backpacking in Patagonia, but they are not enough. *Management* experience is better than *service* experience, *but entrepreneurial experience and spirit trump all others.*

American children appear to be more at home in the world of entrepreneurship. They make market stalls and sell sodas outside their houses. They run "car-wash" or small gardening services. They offer babysitting services. They are pro-active. They look for gaps in the market. Some even under-cut their neighbors. It's fun and rewarding, and very good life experience. They get to understand supply and demand; marketing and selling skills.

Being entrepreneurial is different from making money. The paper round, the supermarket check-out or the "Saturday helping out" job is not really the ticket. Necessary, but not sufficient. The entrepreneurs *start* the business. It is about seeing and responding to an opportunity. It's about doing some elementary math and organizing equipment, and it is about sales. But, most of all, it is about hunger and excitement.

It does not matter particularly whether the enterprise failed – though why precisely it failed may be important. What is equally important is how the budding business person reacted to those problems. Did they treat it as a learning experience, or did it crush them? Did they analyze the cause of the failure and try again? Did they try something else, or were they determined to overcome the problem?

Study the early lives of famous entrepreneurs. Once the PR has been sorted from the facts, what is striking are three things: *first*, how early the entrepreneurial spirit manifested itself; *second*, how often the early entrepreneur failed; *third*, how determined the budding entrepreneur was.

So, where does this entrepreneurial spirit come from? Is it genetic endowment, planned or accidental socialization, or experience? Can you teach it? Entrepreneurs come (literally) in all shapes and sizes. Some go to university; others do not. Left- and right-brain people can succeed as entrepreneurs. Geeks and flaky people can do well.

It is not enough to have a brilliant invention, or spot a wonderful opportunity. It has to be translated into a credible business opportunity. And the goal must not be money. Money is a measure of success, not a goal of enterprise. It is a way of keeping the score. And, of course, it is not to be used for feckless pleasures but, rather, used to sponsor and support new ventures.

The entrepreneurial spirit is a mixture of abilities, traits and values. Only the latter can really be taught, and often as much by example as instruction. Essentialists argue that certain characteristics seem innate. Thus, people are what they are. They don't choose to be gay: they are born gay. Is this true of entrepreneurs? A number of traits could be listed: curiosity, moderate risk-taking, emotional adjustment and resilience, quick-wittedness, perseverance. But can they be taught?

Entrepreneurs are driven, and not by greed: more often, it is the desire to succeed. And, in doing so, they know the lessons of failure. They are not thrown back by rejection, being let down and being double-crossed. It is all part of the game, and they simply resolve not to let it happen next time.

So, look for early and persistent signs of the entrepreneurial spirit. They might be difficult to manage and want quite quickly to run their own show, but they are a special breed who will make a real contribution to most organizations.

25 Executive derailment

It is said that a psychologist going through a famous university library in the late 1980s found 400 books on depression and only two on happiness, provoking him to try to fill the gap. Psychologists seemed to assume that, if you did not have depression, you were happy and that this seemingly trivial subject did not merit research time and effort.

This was all before the positive psychology revolution and the shocking discovery to economists that wealth was very weakly related to health, happiness and well-being. Today, happiness is a serious topic for research.

Now, if you look at the over 50,000 publications with "leadership" in their title, there is equally a conspiracy of neglect. There are autobiographical and biographical studies of leaders, there are "how to" books in droves and there are scholarly works developing theories about the topic.

There are studies of wicked, evil leaders, often written by historians and occasionally psychiatrists, but almost nothing on the "ordinary" wunderkind who lost the plot. It appears to be a taboo subject akin to mental and physical illness in the nineteenth century and homosexuality in the twentieth century. It is not that we refuse to admit that it happens, but nobody is prepared to talk about it.

This would all be understandable, if derailment were rare. But the statistics speak otherwise. There have been 12 papers published over the last 25 years that have made good estimates of management failure. The average of those estimates is 47 percent. Yes, they are estimates and yes there are rather different definitions of failure. Suffice it to say, failure extends from imprisonment (for corruption, and so on) through sacking to resignation long before the contract ended. Management failure occurs when the person appointed to the job fails to deliver the set objectives, often with dire consequences. In short, derailment and disappointment on the part of the job-holder and the appointers and workers are as common as success.

There are observable and hidden costs to all this. The share price tumbles or starts a long decline, but it is the hidden costs that count more. They include demoralized, disengaged, less-productive staff; the loss of intellectual and social capital as turnover of good people increases; and missed business opportunities.

The paradox is that most failures have had very successful careers. The derailed were once the high-flyers. Indeed, what helped them climb to the top also led to their demise. Yet, for many (especially those who appointed them), their failures comes as a great surprise. However, retrospectively, going through the "case history," the clues are all there. Alas, it is only hindsight that is 20/20.

One of the "lessons" of all this is to make someone responsible for selecting out CEOs. The way most appointments are made is to look for evidence of certain attributes or competencies. Usually *more is better*: you can't be too creative, or too customer-focused; it is impossible to be too analytic or have too much integrity . . . or even to be too "good with people." But the evidence suggests the opposite. It is called the "spectrum hypothesis," and suggests that extremes of normality are abnormality. There is no clear dividing line between normality and pathology: it is a spectrum. Thus, very high self-esteem may be seen as clinical narcissism. It is perhaps just as important to have selectors look for evidence of characteristics that they do not want.

The evidence suggests that derailment is a function of three things: very particular personality traits, naïve followers, and particular situations that mean poorly regulated and governed businesses.

First, the potentially derailing leaders. Researchers in this area now talk of the Dark Triad of *sub-clinical psychopathy*. These individuals score high on anti-social and narcissistic personality disorder, whilst having Machiavellian beliefs and behaviors.

The three inter-related features of the dark side are:

- Arrogance, self-centeredness, self-enhancement.
- Duplicity, cynicism, manipulative behavior.
- Emotionally cold, impulsive thrill-seeking and frequently engaged in illegal, dangerous, anti-social behavior.

The argument is this: Dark Triad traits facilitate the exploitation of others in short-term social contexts because:

- Narcissists are proactive, dominant, eager for power.
- Machiavellians can be exploitative charmers.
- Psychopaths have an exploitative nature.

First, "people of the Dark Triad" are high in self-interest but low in empathy. They are therefore not interested in, well-suited for, or good at long-term relationships where a degree of reciprocity is called for. They are found out, so prefer a "hit-and-run" strategy.

But if they are articulate, bright and educated, as well as good-looking, the behaviors associated with the dark triad probably help them climb the greasy pole of business life. The bright ones do well in the city. The less-talented with the dark triad are more likely to turn out to be confidence tricksters, petty criminals and imposters.

People of the dark triad gain a reputation for boldness and self-confidence, pushing through change, cutting back deadwood. They are thought to be adventurous and often mischievous, sometimes bullies. Any names come to mind?

Second, some types of people allow derailing leaders to thrive. We get the politicians and leaders we deserve. It has been said that there are toxic followers. Many have attempted to categorize these into different groups such as bystanders, acolytes, true believers or, more simply, conformers and colluders. Conformers tend to be immature with negative self-concept, whilst colluders are more selfish, ambitious, destructive and openly supportive of toxic tyrants.

What are they like, these toxic board members who even encourage derailing leaders?

Many have low self-esteem that they hope the leader will be able to improve. They also tend to be helpless and fatalistic, expecting the leader to give them power and influence. Toxic leaders reinforce their sense of passivity whilst giving them hope of escape.

Also, toxic followers tend to be morally immature. Their sense of right and wrong is weak and they readily conform to immoral behavior dictated by their leaders. Vulnerable, immature, impressionable adults make good followers of strong but destructive leaders. Under-socialized or morally undeveloped people are happy to endorse the violence of toxic leaders.

Toxic followers yearn for rank and status and power: people ambitious for status and land/*lebensraum* make better followers. The more they see there is psychological and material profit to be had following, the quicker and more happily they follow.

Finally, they share the values and beliefs of their leader, which are often fundamentalists and based on some in-group superiority. Simply, followers who share world views with those of the destructive leader are naturally more likely to follow them.

But the social, economic and legal climate can help or hinder the dark-triad leader. They do best in situations of flux and instability. Political, economic and social instability are very frightening. Toxic leaders exploit fluidity, advocating radical means to restore peace, harmony and progress. They are granted excessive authority and power that they are reluctant to relinquish. Next, the more people feel personally threatened, the more internal and external enemies they see around, then the happier they are to follow toxic leaders who promise them security.

Third, dark triad leaders do best in cultures that are uncomfortable around ambiguity and uncertainty; those that have elaborate rules and rituals that offer easy solutions to complex problems are easier to control. Further, the more there is disparity between rich and poor, educated and uneducated, high and low status, the more the toxic leader thrives.

But the most important factor is where corporate governance is weak: where power is centralized, and those monitoring authority and responsibility are silenced. This is like removing the internal audit from the organization. It means the end of constraint and monitoring.

The issue is always the appropriate balance between over-regulation versus under-regulation. There is a cost to supplying the information required for good corporate governance. It can be that paying too much attention to internal auditing and the supply of accounting information taxes the organization too heavily.

Some leaders feel, quite rightly, that they are handicapped – even trapped – by the requirements of corporate governance. They feel they cannot act quickly or boldly enough to do what has to be done. They see governance not as a wise system of checks and balances but, rather, as a suffocating system of bureaucracy that leads to long-term failure.

Often, business and political leaders have significant decisional and behavioral latitude. But can this discretion, this latitude, be a significant derailer? Discretion is freedom, freedom is power, and power can corrupt. Some senior jobs involve a great deal of responsibility, but not much discretion. Rules and regulations, ever-watchful shareholders and the media, in addition to financial and other constraints, simply reduce the opportunities of the grown-ups to misbehave, make mistakes or simply "lose the plot."

Good managers are characterized by various phenomena. Often, they tend to pro-actively seek feedback from trusted, honest observers throughout their career to monitor how they are doing. Next, they seek out opportunities to grow, develop, learn or upgrade important skills. They also seek a formal or informal coach or mentor to help them through times of acute change or transition. In short, they seek out sources of assessment, challenges and support.

Those prone to derailment do not do this. Through hubris, anxiety or lack of insight, they have to be given "developmental" assignments and coerced to go. They might go on short, taught leadership programs, but few cite those events later as crucial ingredients in their development. They need opportunities to examine their style, strengths and weaknesses with intensive and honest feedback.

Paradoxically perhaps, an early career failure or mishap can be an excellent learning experience, so that mistakes are not repeated. Coaching for executives can help a great deal. Some organizations have prescribed mentoring where every manager at a certain level is mentored by a person above them. Not all derailment can be prevented. However, much can be done to help the stressed leader who is crossing over the thin line between poor management and pathology.

The cost of derailment is high – for the individual manager and his/her family, peers and subordinates and for the company as a whole. Often, derailment is quite unexpected. Yet, nearly always, a more careful and critical review of derailed leaders' biographies contain all the cues that derailment might occur. By then, it is too late.

Organizations can reduce, rather than prevent or eliminate, the prospect of their senior leaders and managers derailing by ensuring good governance and strong management processes. Leaders need enough freedom to maneuver but not unlimited power.

All leaders work with "top teams," called "boards" or "cabinets" or whatever. These groups can easily become highly dysfunctional and, themselves, be a cause of management derailment. It is desirable to have someone monitor the health of boards from time to time.

There are many stages where derailment may be addressed. The most obvious are recruitment and selection. There is now much more interest in this issue, and excellent psychometrically validated tests are available with which to evaluate the dark side of personality. These can indicate possible areas of concern about leaders' behavior when put under pressure, which they inevitably are.

Coaching and mentoring can help. Paradoxically, those who need it most also resist it most and benefit from it least. It takes a highly skilled coach to confront a very senior manager/leader and help him or her to avoid derailment.

26 Four legs good; two legs bad

Management writers and gurus seem to favor the old "compare and contrast" school of examining issues. One favorite is the "old world–new world" distinction. The old world we look back on is a sad place of inefficiency, bureaucracy and technological naïvety. But we are now in a fluid, electronic age of many possibilities.

Over 30 years ago, it became popular to differentiate between two types of senior people in organizations. If you are pretentious, you call it "transformational vs. transactional." If you are not, you call it "leaders and managers." And if you like slogans, it is about "doing the right thing" as opposed to "doing things right." You manage things, you lead people.

To help the compare and contrast game, a number of writers have come up with tables that summarize the differences. They are, for the most part, evidence-free nonsense. Worse, to emphasize differences (that really exist), they paint a picture of the dim, backward, inflexible manager in opposition to the heroic enviable visionary.

A flip through half a dozen popular management books (if you are a dull manager) or a quick search on the web (if you are a modern leader) yields many of those tables. Consider some of the traits and behavioral styles associated with management: controlling, reactive, forcing, regimenting, stifling. Leaders are, of course, inspiring, motivating, and democratic. They are also supposed to be enabling, freeing and releasing. Managers, you see, are authoritarians who have subordinates, whilst leaders, who are charismatic, have followers. Managers are task-focused and risk-averse, whilst leaders are people that are focused and seek risk.

Remind me to ask my airplane pilot and heart surgeon if they are leaders. I certainly hope not.

Leaders seem to be such heroes. They give credit and take blame, whilst managers do the opposite. Equally, leaders take risks and break rules, whilst poor dull, conservative, managers minimize risks and seem to have huge fun making more and more rules. Leaders are people of the heart, and managers are people of the head. Leaders sell, managers tell.

But it gets worse. Managers, it seems, have neither imagination nor creativity, or a moral conscience. They perpetuate group conflict and became very anxious when there is any disorder. They only "tinker" with changes and, themselves, have low work engagement. They are punishment-oriented, rigid, drill sergeants. They are mechanistic, compartmentalizing, obedience-demanding dullards.

But on the white charger is our "dear leader." He (or she) overflows with energy and imagination; fizzes with electric creativity. They enjoy chaos but are super-empathic, intuitive and interpersonally skilled. They are rewarding, empowering and networking. And they are holistic, systemic mentors. They are probably "greenies" to boot, nourishing people and environment alike.

Enough! Neither stereotype exists, though many people at supervisory level are recruited and rewarded for a spot of command and control behavior. And that's a good thing. Most people want them to ensure the supermarket shelves are stocked and the trains run on time.

All the "four legs good, two legs bad" tables never explain how and why people become leaders and managers. Have leaders never been managers? How did they cope? Do they suddenly switch sides?

Managers seem so awful. No one ever would aspire to be a manager. You certainly would never want to invite one to dinner. Obsessional train-spotters, if you believe this guff.

But, then, how likable are these leader-johnnies? They seem a bit like adolescent tear-aways. Full of impractical ideas, risk-taking extroverts, iconoclasts, possibly self-obsessed. The leader is Jamie Oliver. Well, maybe.

Leaders are quirky geniuses. Managers are solid citizens who keep the show on the road. Managers, then, would certainly make poor leaders, or would they? Does it not depend on the sector they are working in, and the context?

27 The gaff-prone CEO

Everyone makes the occasional gaff. We make mistakes; say something we don't mean, muddle up the names, forget crucial facts, and have funny slips of the tongue. But most of us aren't in the spotlight – we're not being continually recorded in the media by cameras, microphones and observant journalists. Those that are have to endure years of humiliation as cheap-and-cheerful programs are replayed with their slips-of-the-tongue or tired-and-emotional outbursts captured on tape.

Politicians are highly-skilled performers. They often know precisely how *not* to answer a question; how to spin not so much a yarn, as an uncomfortable fact. They are superb, if predictable, attributors: able to attribute all success to their own ability, effort and intervention – but all failure to opposition strategies, market forces, or enemy government. Politicians only seem gaff-prone because they appear in the media so often. Tired, poorly-informed, off their guard, they are still recorded. And these "mere snippets" are replayed again and again until it makes them look particularly and unusually gaff-prone.

It does not take many gaffs to have a major effect, as Gerald Ratner found. And the outgoing head of BP may not be too good either. Gaffs come in many kinds. *First*, there is the delicious Freudian slip, the parapraxis. Here, the person says what they **really** (unconsciously) hope, want, feel, rather than what they should be saying. Simply one small wrong word can change everything and lead to what old Sigmund called "the royal road to the unconscious."

Second, there is the joker. They may be brilliant wordsmiths like Boris Johnson, or rather cruder models who see either the funny side or farcical side of something that quickly backfires.

Third, there is the ill-prepared gaff. This is where the person, supremely confident in their power to "wing it," stumbles and falls, and shows their ignorance.

Fourth, there is the supercilious gaff when the person haughtily dismisses or disparages something. This can readily offend. Better always to go with English (insincere?) self-deprecation than this.

Fifth, ignorance of political correctness, where (often) some old buffer uses an expression, however common in their day, that is now totally "*verboten*." A member of the House of Lords used "The N in the woodpile" and was ritually rebuked.

It is the job of CEO to face the press, the shareholders and the company from time-to-time; explaining, reassuring, calming. They are the figurehead of the company, the guardian of the share price, the embodiment of the brand.

One way to prevent or at least minimize the risk of gaffs is to practice. Better still, have a skilful speech writer. Recall the surprise when David Cameron, current British Prime Minister, abandoned the autocues and dared speak without notes to the audience. Of course, what looks like spontaneity could be word-perfect memorization. But it can be difficult reading other peoples words, however clear they are. Over time, great speech writers learn the rhythms of their speaker, and the typical metaphors and similes they use. Yet, that takes time and, after all, CEOs do have to attend charity events, local radio interviews and the like where they are not prepared.

Many CEOs can't afford scriptwriters. The personnel relations department may advise on dress and which venues and events carry most impact, but they rarely rise to having a full- or even part-time speech writer onboard. So, CEOs make gaffs: some small, amusing and forgivable; others, terrifying in their consequences. Possibly. But CEOs know they are occasionally called on for very important interviews or speeches to "steady-the-boat," put "backbone in the troops" or "charm the shareholders."

The CEOs most gaff-prone might be:

- **Impulsive, hubristic types**: come across as a lethal combination of cocky and unprepared. They can seem not to understand the problem whilst simultaneously having a naïve belief that they can fix it. They don't prepare enough.
- **Technical specialists**: make mistakes when they are asked to account for issues outside their area of expertise. Financial wizards may be very naïve about people. Inventor-boffins, childlike in their understanding of economics.
- **Nervous performers**: as evident in the *Dragon's Den*, some have learnt their lines (their proposition) but they are overwhelmed by the lights, cameras and celebrities. They stumble, mutter and leave out crucial points whilst inserting nonsense.

- **Bored humorists**: Kenneth Williams became bored with theater – eight times a week saying the same old stuff. So, he adlibbed to amuse himself. The clever, naughty schoolboy inside the CEO occasionally pops up to the delight of the listeners and the gaff-hunters.
- **Over-promoted Mr Average**: sometimes, the CEO has got to the top more by connections, luck or guile than ability, and it shows with their more modest vocabulary, their colloquial turn of phrase and their occasional inability to understand questions.

Gaffs might be fun for the observer. They are the stuff of ever-popular blooper programs; but too many and too frequent gaffs can end a CEO's career.

28 Good advice

The Last Lecture (Pausch, 2007) by an American academic who died aged 47 was an Internet sensation watched by millions. It was a televised lecture given by an engineering academic after he was diagnosed with inoperable, certainly fatal, pancreatic cancer.

It was characterized by good humor, not mawkish sentimentality. But its aim – disguised to the last moment – was to give advice to his children and to give them something to remember him by.

It lead him to fame and a "ghost-written" – or, rather, "dictated and editor-assisted" – book. Various charities have been started in his name and the cause of death has, no doubt, received a boost in funds.

People have noted that his advice for a happy, contented life where you can fulfill your childhood ream is hardly new. He advises: "tell the truth," "apologize for your mistakes" and "have fun." Hardly awe-inspiring stuff: but the way he expressed it, and the conditions under which he spoke and wrote, gave it poignancy. You have heard it all before; you know it to be (mostly) true; and you can't quite think of why you don't (always, sometimes or even ever) follow that advice.

So, why not your own list? Say, five maxims to live by; advice for your children; the wisdom of the ages. Whatever. Here are mine:

Carpe Diem

That's Latin for "Seize the day," "Life is not a dress rehearsal," "Use it or lose it" or "Time is precious." Everyone who has had a brush with mortality speaks of living life more intensely.

This means making, finding and using opportunities. It means acting, not deferring or dithering. It means fully taking part. It means *seize the day*, not plan the day, chill out, coast along. Pitching up and pitching in. It means "being there," wherever you are and whatever you are doing. You can do everything with more mindfulness; more concentration. You can make opportunities to shop, explore, challenge and listen. They used to say "Today is the first day of the rest of your life." Easier to think of it as your last.

Explore, exploit, explode your talents

It is particularly sad to see people with real talent waste their talents. Talents as normally distributed, and there are many different sorts – talents in math and music, mentoring, as well as therapy, teaching and triathlons. But how do you find out what you are good at? This often happens by accident. Some take to their graves manifold talents that they simply never explored. To be good at something, to know what it is, to share and exploit it is terribly important. Best to find out and exploit talents than work on weaknesses. And the best ways to find out what you are good at? Have a go at things. Try it. Difficult – yes: people can and do discover very late in life that they were good at things and they had no idea.

Kindness is reciprocated

Generosity of spirit is a virtue. Altruism, empathy, kindness or whatever bonds us together. But it always, in the long run, gets repaid. Another synonymous expression is "What goes around comes around." Exploit others and, eventually, you won't have any friends at all. Sure, there will be those eager to exploit generosity of spirit or wallet. There will be time-wasters and victims sorry for themselves and constantly wanting reassurance.

But the majority of people respond very well to all small and big acts of kindness. What, after all, do you leave behind? Care, compassion and kindness are at the heart of the human condition. You won't be remembered for your possessions or, worse your, possessiveness. But you may for the little and big kindnesses that often cost so little.

Inspiration comes from perspiration

If you work hard at what you both like doing and are good at it, it's not hard work at all. But there are times we need perseverance, dogged hard work and dutiful conscientiousness.

Most skills take considerable investment in practice. Long hours of forsaken leisure and pleasure in order to do things well and properly. Few achievements in art and science come without diligence and sacrifice. This is equally true of creativity. Inspiration occurs often in the incubation stage, after much work has been done.

Hard work has killed few people in the last 100 years. Hard work – not for its own sake and as a substitute for other things – is always repaid.

Look back but move on

Yes, life is a journey. There is no final destination except the grave. But, depending on your theology, that too is not the end. It's about how you travel. Important to know where you have come from. We are all forced and molded in some great iron-works, but we can and do change, progress and develop. But too much looking at the past, particularly with regret, changes nothing. The past is another country: they do things differently there.

We have a past, a present and a future. The latter two are important. Live in the present with an eye to the future. But it's important to have goals, targets and aims. It's important to modify them and re-evaluate them, for they are the great beacons on the map or the lighthouse in the sea.

29 Half a mo: thin slices of behavior

Do first impressions count? Of course they do. The beautifully-cut Italian suit, the unkempt hair, the limp handshake. We prepare ourselves for job interviews to impress. Dress, grooming and non-verbals carry weight.

How often are interviewers struck – indeed, almost put off their task – by the interviewee's loud socks, unfortunate tick or bold bling? What messages do tattoos now carry? Once the adornment almost exclusively of sailors and prisoners, they now seem to be the chosen "body art" of respectable middle-class people from "nice homes" and "good schools."

Most serious interlocutors like to believe that they are not distracted by "superficialities." Everyone knows that you should not "judge a book by its cover." Snap judgments can be bad judgments. The task is to discover the candidate's real abilities, competencies, motivation and such like.

We know a great deal about selection errors and biases – often from personal experience. We know that we rate as competent, confident and likeable those people who are similar to ourselves in background, demography and values. We know the power of physical attraction: what is beautiful is good. We also fall for good looks. We might not do palm- or mind-reading, but we sure do face- and body-reading. We know that one piece of negative information (school expulsion, trouble with the police, serious illness) can outweigh 10 pieces of positive information.

One study even showed the perfume a candidate wore influenced hiring decisions. The same actress – wearing either a popular, unpopular or no perfume – was interviewed as a temp by dozens of males. She was rated more able, honest and efficient if she wore the popular (sexy) perfume, rated by the interviewers some time before in an unrelated task.

More worrying is the research that shows that the first impression changes the interviewer's behavior and, subsequently, the candidate's behavior in return. That is, the quick reaction to a person (their stunning beauty, their shocking scruffiness) unwittingly causes the interviewer to act, appear or behave in ways consistent with those impressions. These, in turn, influence the candidate's behavior. This can even happen with pre-interview information, which is why some organizations have banned photographs and CVs, instead, providing short, sparse application forms.

It has been demonstrated that pre-interview impressions and ratings influence how the interview is conducted, and also the outcome ratings.

So, we go about having structured interviews where every candidate is asked the same questions in the same way and in the same order to reduce bias. We should know why we are asking the questions, what information we are trying to extract, and why it is relevant to the job. Thus, both men and women are (or are not) asked about children and about IT skills.

We know that some impressions can be easily changed. In a celebrated study undertaken quite some time ago (Argyle and Mchendry, 1971), it was found that when people wore attractive, modern spectacles they were rated as more intelligent than if not wearing spectacles. But this only applied to photographs: on video, their vocabulary outweighed the face. We have also known about primacy and recency effects for over 80 years. That is, the information that comes first and last in a series is more memorable than all the information in the middle.

But how much information do you need on someone to make a reasonable judgment? This is more than asking how long the interview should be. It is about the quality and quantity of data required to make a good judgment.

We read of people marrying 10 days after they first met, and we now have "speed dating." Surely, one of the most important judgments we make is in partner selection. After all, a partner will, to a large extent, be our legacy – the propagator of our genes, co-creator of our whole lives. So, what can be gained through speed dating? The answer, of course, lies not so much in the speed, as in the questions.

There is a surprising and quite fascinating new branch of psychology concerned with the histology of social behaviors. It is better called "thin slices" psychology. The question is: what information could you possibly obtain from a 10-second video of an individual talking to camera? Or, even simpler, a photograph of their bedroom or study. The literature in this area is pretty surprising.

This is how the studies are done. Take a group of people varying in anything you like – race, age, ability. Then test them thoroughly. Give them IQ tests and personality tests, put them through rigorous assessment centers, find out what their teachers and peers and workmates really think about them. Even interview them. Do not stop until you are pretty clear in your knowledge of the individual. Then, video an open-ended interview, asking questions such as "Tell me a little about yourself," "What would you describe as your strengths or assets?," "What is your most unique quality?," "Describe your friends," "Why should we choose you over the other candidates?"

Now take that video, starting from the first greeting between interviewer and interviewee, and edit it down to a series of 30-second clips. Or be more radical: edit to 10 seconds. So, you should have, say, 30 clips of exactly 10 seconds on 30 people you know very well because they have been thoroughly assessed. Now, show them to a panel of judges who make individual ratings on those features that you have measured. Judges rate how clever (intelligent) or extroverted or creative the individual is. They may rate emotional intelligence, neuroticism or conscientiousness. Any attribute is acceptable, as it is the one you have objectively measured.

There are variations of the method. One is to film a real interview by a trained expert interviewer (or panel of interviewers) who makes a series of ratings including yes/no, select/reject. But 10 seconds of that interview (which may last between 30 and 45 minutes) is shown to experimental participants – the naïve judges. Here, the study looks at the similarity between the real interviewers and the naïve people who only saw 10 seconds of that interview. The question is what they can and do "pick up." How much information is carried in a (very) thin slice of behavior?

The results are astonishing. So it has been true all along. The first seconds of an interview do count. You can sum up a person pretty well quite quickly. No need for hours and hours of social contact to understand an individual reasonably well.

30   Hire positive people

The advent of positive psychology and the shocking realization by economists that money is only weakly related to well-being has lead to a flurry of books on happiness.

One British government seemed convinced enough to consider "happiness" lessons as part of the syllabus. We know what brings happiness: health, a sunny disposition, good friends and relationships, helping others out.

But the jury is out with regard to teaching happiness. We all know the *heart-sinking* person, the pessimist, the complainer, the gloom-and-doom monger. Whatever happens to them, they remain negative, helpless and hopeless.

By contrast, we know the *life-enhancers*. They may be called "sunny" or "bonny" or simply "optimists." They bounce back from adversity and remain resolutely positive.

They are, for the most part, stable extroverts, whilst the heart-sinkers are unstable introverts. And there is not much one can do about one's personality. You are what you are. We know that people do not change much over time: we do become a little less neurotic and extroverted and open-to-experience, but more agreeable and conscientious over time. But these personality traits are remarkably stable despite what happens to us, be it winning the lottery or a terrible accident leaving us paralyzed.

And those who have studied the role of personality, emotion and mood have found, not surprisingly, that happy people, simply defined as those who experience positive emotions, are more successful at work.

Compared with unhappy people – but matched on other criteria such as education, experience, skills, the data reveal the following:

- Happier people get better jobs – those with more autonomy, variety and meaning
- Happier CEOs have happier people working for them
- Happier people show better job performance
- Happier people make more money.

These findings occur across jobs, from counselors to cricketers, and in different countries, studying everyone from German business people to Malaysian farmers.

So what explains these findings? Why is there a connection between positive moods, a sense of well-being, happiness and work success? There seem to be various different factors.

- **Focus and distraction**: unhappy people are too prone to taking their eye off the ball at work. They tend to be more self-obsessed and not as vigilant about the needs of others, be they colleagues or customers.
- **Memory**: the mood conjuring effect is well-established. People in a good mood recall more positive things, and vice versa. Hence, we get virtuous and vicious cycles. Positive people recall happy customers and co-operative peers; unhappy people never let go of their negative experiences. Positive people put in more effort to achieve the positive results they will recall.
- **Decision-making**: people with sunny dispositions make better decisions: they are faster, more accurate and more inclusive. Unhappy people are too "hung up" about small, irrelevant issues and alienate those who are trying to help them. Optimistic people believe that problems are solvable and that they can (with help) make good decisions. The pessimists are hapless, hopeless and helpless ... and often either procrastinate, or make poorer decisions than the optimists.
- **Evaluating others**: we all know bosses are best avoided when they are in a bad mood, particularly for annual appraisals. People in a good mood are more encouraging, more forgiving, more tolerant of others and their "little foibles." Negative moods are associated with blaming and attacking others, rather than helping them. Negative people make bad colleagues and team members.
- **Co-operating**: good moods make people more generous, more co-operative, more helpful. People in a good mood tend to deflate crises and resolve conflicts. Those in a bad mood increase conflict.

Read self-help books from Dale Carnegie to the present day. Read Baden Powell on *Scouting for Boys*. Read books on sales techniques. They all give the same advice with respect to being happy: "Kick the 'im' out of impossible!"

No one likes an unpredictable, moody boss, colleague or customer. This instability is called "neuroticism" and is associated with anxiety, depression and hypochondriasis. We also wisely shy away from people who shy away from us. This is called "introversion." We quite happily use personality tests in selection, so why not use them to select in dispositionally happy people and select out unhappy people? Should optimism be a competency?

We can fake happiness for interviewers, but people do acquire a reputation for their emotional stability and mood regulation. You could obtain that information from referees. How Happy is X as a person? Rate this person on an Optimist/Pessimist scale.

So, what to do if you are a pessimist? The happiness gurus do give advice. They suggest that you:

- Accept that enduring happiness doesn't come from worldly and materialistic success.
- Take control of your time, and aim for a little progress each day.
- Act happy, because going through the motions can trigger the emotions you need.
- Seek work and leisure pursuits that engage your natural strengths and skills.
- Join social groups that reflect your interests, values and passions.
- Get enough exercise and sleep every day.
- Give priority to close relationships, by affirming others and sharing together.
- Focus on others more than yourself.
- Keep a record of good things that happened to you (gifts, blessings).

So, hire happy people: working with successful optimists may be the best thing you can do.

31 How management style leads directly to profit and loss

The service–profit chain "theory" first published as a Harvard Business School Review paper, and later as a successful book, was based on a causal chain model that led from customer satisfaction to profit.

It showed a causal path that went like this: internal service quality (processes, procedures and management style) related directly to employee satisfaction, which drove both retention and productivity. These, in turn, drove the value proposition or the service concept for customers. This subsequently led to customer loyalty, which influenced both revenue growth and profitability.

On the extreme left was the ultimate goal: profit. This was, in the service business, a function of repeat business by happy customers. It was the excellent ("delight, don't just satisfy me") service that did the trick. And this, in turn, was driven by good managers, a healthy adaptive culture and good management practice. Good managers chose and motivated good staff, who consistently delivered the golden goose. And management style is determined primarily by the manager's ability, personality and values

There are some crucial concepts in this model for sustained profitability:

Customer loyalty and satisfaction: companies with profit and growth are characterized by a large number of loyal repeat customers who seek out the specific product and services of the company. Loyal customers are more likely to tell others about their loyalty than "just" satisfied customers. Customer loyalty is driven by employees. Managers often have little direct contact with customers, but their direct influence on employees is very significant.

They have to cultivate a productive employee, but shape and develop a cohesive team of individuals who share a passion for the business. Some customers defect from organizations; others are indifferent; some are affectionate. It is only the latter that are really loyal. A satisfied customer is not automatically a loyal customer unless they have no choice. Only the highly-satisfied customers become loyal. Customer expectations change all the time. If a company wants to maintain that loyalty, it has to continually get better and out-perform its rivals.

Value: satisfaction depends on the company's ability to create value for the customer. Value means that the customer has gained *more* from the product than he thinks it is worth. Value often has an *emotional* aspect that makes an experience particularly *memorable* for the customer. The key to create value is the ability to *bond emotionally*. Value is created by loyal employees.

Employee productivity: satisfied and loyal employees are far more productive. Value has to do with the employee's ability to act on the wishes and needs of the customers and to find solutions. Productive employees usually have a higher degree of product knowledge and customer knowledge. Thus, employees who have served quite a few years in the company usually are much more productive than new employees.

Employee loyalty: employee loyalty is driven by enthusiasm and satisfaction; engagement and commitment. To be able to create excited customers and contribute to memorable experiences, you need to be excited as an employee as well. This implies that the employees must be happy with their jobs to have what it takes to meet the customers' complex and immediate needs. Loyalty refers to considerate employees who stay long in the company and have great knowledge of the customers and the processes and culture within the company.

Employee satisfaction: employee loyalty is driven by employee satisfaction. In the same way that customer loyalty is driven by engagement, rather than just satisfaction, employee loyalty depends on the same principle. Employee "satisfaction" is not the same as "engagement," which is more difficult and much more complex. In the service–profit chain, employee satisfaction is a result of "internal quality" which, again, relates to a number of elements that have to be present to ensure employee satisfaction.

Managerial style: managers lead as a function of their ability, personality and values. These usually determine the sort of experience they have had before, during and outside work. A good manager can inspire and engage and motivate as quickly and thoroughly as a bad one can do the opposite. Even if the systems in place and the product are not ideal, good managers can get the very best out of their staff

It is important to recognize that leadership and management style underlie the chain's success. Individual managers motivate and reward; they create and sustain the healthy, productive culture. Thus, the questions for leaders are: Do all employees know who their customers are? And, perhaps more importantly, Are they satisfied with the technical and personal support and direction that they receive on the job? The more the leadership is energetic, participatory, caring, listening and coaching-oriented vs. elitist, removed, supervisory, the better. And what determines how a person manages is their personality, ability and values.

Exit interviews demonstrate that people don't resign from jobs, they resign because of individual managers. And appraisal interviews show that people stay engaged and productive because of individual managers. That is why managerial selection and promotion is so important. In short, managers make all the difference: they start the chain reaction.

32   How to be happy

It pays to be happy. Happy people live longer and, by definition, happier lives. They make better decisions and have more fulfilling relationships. They also make more money, being as much a consequence of happiness as a cause.

The psychology of happiness attempts to answer some very fundamental questions pursued over the years by philosophers, theologians and politicians. The *first* series of questions is really about definition and measurement of happiness; the *second* is about why certain groups are as happy or unhappy as they are; and the *third* concerns what a person should do (or not do) to increase happiness.

The research evidence suggests that happy people have strong immune systems. They tend to be more successful at work and have better personal relationships at work and outside. They are more attractive to others. They seem to like themselves more than unhappy people and to cope better with life's setbacks. Happy people make better decisions and tend to be more creative. Unhappy people seem to waste time and effort being vigilant for signs of failure. This saps their energy.

There is evidence that subjective well-being is partly inherited. Twin studies have shown that, just as people inherit a propensity or predisposition for depression, so they do likewise for happiness. But environmental factors inevitably play a part, particularly early family home environments, which can mark us for the future. We also know that, although people can experience events that cause them extreme happiness or unhappiness in the short term, they tend to return to their normal happiness levels relatively quickly.

It seems that some societies and individuals are simply happier than others: thus, Latin nations seen happier than Pacific Rim nations. Several factors seem to relate to overall national happiness: the wealth, stability and democratic nature of the society in which people live; and the social norms and conventions governing the desirability of experiencing positive and negative emotions. The evidence shows that dire poverty certainly makes people unhappy but, at the other extreme, great wealth has little effect on subjective well-being. Studies also show that the more materialistic, the less happy the individual. The happiest people all seem to have good friends.

So, even if you do not inherit a "sunny disposition" or a family fortune, you can become happier. The gurus in this game have made the following observations:

- Don't count on money. Wealth is only weakly related to happiness both within and across nations, particularly when income is above the poverty level. You become no happier after reaching an income of around US$50,000 per annum.
- Don't count on retail therapy or eating out to bring happiness. Activities that make people happy in small doses – such as shopping or good food – do not lead to fulfillment in the long term, indicating that these have quickly diminishing returns.
- Get creative and let your juices flow. Engaging in an experience that produces "flow" is really gratifying and happy-making. Flow is experienced when one's skills are sufficient for a challenging activity, in the pursuit of a clear goal, when immediate self-awareness disappears, and sense of time is distorted.
- Be thankful for what you have, and what others have done for you. People who express gratitude on a regular basis have better physical health, optimism and well-being; progress toward goals; and help others more.
- Get on with it. Happiness is a journey, not a destination. It is a process not a goal. Trying to maximize personal happiness can lead to unhappiness. Act happy to be happy.
- Watch the Good Samaritan; observe selfless volunteers. People who witness others perform good deeds experience an emotion called "elevation," and this motivates them to perform their own good deeds. In this sense, happiness spreads.
- Learn to see the glass half-full. Optimism can protect people from distress. Optimism is self-fulfilling ... as is pessimism. Whether you believe you can or you can't, you are right.
- Start early: people who report more positive emotions in young adulthood live longer and healthier lives.
- Take the knocks: healthy human development can take place under conditions of even great adversity due to a resilience that is common and completely ordinary.
- Scribble away your woes. Individuals who write about traumatic events are physically healthier than control groups who do not. Writing about

life goals is significantly less distressing than writing about trauma, and is associated with enhanced well-being.

Should happiness be a competency at work? Should employers seek out inspiring, spirit-lifting, life-enhancing types, and reject gloom-mongering heart-sinkers? Why not? Is happiness easy to fake at an interview? Probably. But ask a referee to rate a person's base level of happiness and they will have no problems in doing so accurately.

So, is this discrimination? Certainly. Is it unfair? Only to those who want to work with pessimists. Is it illegal? Not yet!

Happiness needs to be passed around. It can be (partly) acquired. It is a social good and a business asset. Seek out, reward and encourage the happy.

33 The identification of high-flyers

What happened to the hype about talent management? The recruitment, selection, development and deployment of *high-flyers* was, supposedly, the most important thing companies could do to thrive and survive ... or so we were told by the gurus. The issue was finding the elusive wunderkind.

Was all that bull market rhetoric including similar concepts such as the *war for talent*. Recall the now almost preposterous notion that there was a limited *and* decreasing number of super-talented young people who were the leaders of the future, and that companies had to fight hard to get them. Fight hard, of course, meant giving them incredible (dare one say "banker-like") packages to lure them to join the company. But worth it: they are saviors!

Now the brightest-of the-bright seem to be stacking shelves or babbling in call-centers. And talent management seems to have quietly gone off the agenda in many companies. But, even when it was all the rage – and it will return, the whole business was fraught with problems.

There were essentially **three** important issues. The *first* was the criteria by which someone became classified, "honored" or labeled with the term. The most common policy was to have a **performance–potential grid**. High-flyers were the few with a record of high performance and who were judged also to have high potential. Consultants and managers always favor these 2×2 grids for decision-making.

The appeal of the grid is that it is prescriptive about what you do with people, given where they in the map.

The *second* problem for talent management is equally interesting. Should the list of the chosen ones, the high-flyers, be public? Should we know who is in the "gold group," or whatever it is called? This can cause two undesirable consequences: smugness and complacency in those who made it; and envious, demoralizing fury in those who did not. A double-whammy – because you simultaneously let the striving relax and upset all the others. You also have to then explain the criteria by which people are, or are not, put in the group – landing you back with problem 1, which is also possibly a secret.

So, why not let the classification be secret (to senior managers, or head HR people)? Will this cause more or less trouble? People will notice that they are treated differently: some will be invited to expensive business school short courses and others will not. And secrets will out, which often makes things worse for what it says about senior management – and HR, in particular.

Third, there is the problem of social mobility in and out of the exclusive club. How porous is the membrane – in the sense that those once classified as high-flyers lose their status, and those who did not quite make it are reclassified? And, if so, what are the criteria for losing membership (failing to meet key performance indicators or key responsibilities and accountability targets?) or being reclassified? Of course, there will always be some movement but, given the very dodgy nature of the classification in the first place, one might expect a good deal of change such that those judged high-flyers cease and those lesser beings being regarded (now) as high-flyers. This partly solves the complacency and jealousy problem above.

Many people still hate intelligence tests, particularly selection at school. Many still go on about the 11-plus exam (taken in the UK by 11-year-olds to determine what type of high school they would go to) that seemed to decide your fate as a pre-adolescent. They say you got labeled and often mislabeled. It was all so unfair and unjust: it wasted talent.

So, how is talent management different, except perhaps that the criteria by which one is labeled are less reliable and valid?

34   Implicit assumptions

A high-flyer – anointed, fast-tracked and well-thought-of – suddenly derails. A "steady hand" from middle management loses the plot. A long-term employee, often thought of as a plodder and a dullard, pulls off yet another sales job. Why?

Managers from the real world, like academics from their lofty ivory towers, have theories. They have theories of personality and ability. What are the signs to look for of good, great and poor workers? How to manage each differently and whether, if at all, they can change?

Managers' implicit assumptions were written about 50 years ago in the famous Theory X and Theory Y distinction. It was a sort of Hobbs vs. Rousseau contest. Workers are inherently lazy, feckless, shirkers, who have to be cajoled – even forced – to do a good day's work. Or else, they are potentially self-motivated, productive, enthusiasts who simply need a little encouragement.

The latest work has focused rather on the *rigidity* vs. *malleability* of worker attributes. Put simply: Can people change? And, if so, how easily? Again, there are two extremes. The *fixed mindset* and the *growth mindset*, also called "entity" and "incremental" theorists. The fixed mindset types believe ability, motivation and personality are pretty well set. You can't teach an old dog new tricks. What you see is what you get. No training or therapy or even trauma will change a person's "deepest" attributes.

"Piffle, balderdash and bunkum," shout the growth mindset managers. "Of course people can change, develop and learn. Evidence is all around you. Training works, people can develop." As many women say on their wedding day, "I'll alter him", not "aisle, altar, hymn."

Of course, these are extreme positions and they look upon one another somewhat skeptically. The growth chappies see the fixed chappies as cynical pessimists, whilst they perceive their opposites as naïve time- and money-wasters. Fixed mindset managers see themselves as tough realists, pragmatic and stoical, rather than fatalistic. Growth mindset people see themselves as custodians, developers and drawers-out of talent, potential and skills.

One rather difficult question is, who is right: when, why, what about and how much? Another interesting question concerns, how managers who hold these different positions act.

Various studies have looked at how these assumptions affect performance appraisals. Fixed mindset managers form early and firm impressions of others, which they tend not to change. Growth mindset people are happier with inconsistency, ambiguity.

One study looked at nuclear power managers with both views. They watched a video of an employee, at first, performing poorly and then performing rather well in a negotiation situation. Results showed the growth managers recognized and rated the (real) improvement much more than the mindset managers.

It seems the growth mindset types are optimistically eager to see evidence of change, growth and learning. And what if employees show no evidence of learning? Fixed-minded managers say, "I told you." Growth-mindset types search desperately for evidence to support their position. Mindsets, then, anchor judgments.

What would you prefer your manager to have? The answer of course is a fixed-mindset, but fixed on the positive – the halo, not the horns, effect. Some workers do feel de-motivated, resentful, even alienated when they put effort into, and do, change but have it go unrecognized by the skeptical fixed-mindset boss.

Those with fixed-mindsets are loath to invest in training. They are more likely to favor punishment over education as a means to improve performance.

And so, ironically, how, if you want to, can you change a fixed-mindset manager's view? A sort of "physician heal thyself" question. You try scientific evidence to the contrary. Or counter-attitudinal thinking, where they are asked to think of when and why people have changed their attitudes, abilities and motivation. You could try a bit of dissonance by getting them to share the (albeit few) incidences where they did admit growth.

But then, equally, one may want to inject a little sanity into the high-spending, pro-coaching, training-addicted manager who believes everything is changeable.

You can train skills and modify behavior. You can – with time, patience, and even luck – change a person's view of themselves. You can't do much with their temperament; or change their basic ability level.

35 Incentivizing presentism

Public health professionals, politicians and the general public have taken a great deal of interest in the result of medical research into financially incentivizing people to change their health-related behavior. Pay people to stop smoking, lose weight, visit their doctor, take some exercise.

Whilst there is a passionate debate about whether the taxes on tobacco and alcohol "pay for" the extra medical cost of diseases (lung cancer, cirrhosis of the liver) associated with those products, there is now a new debate on when, whether and why we should pay people to stop unhealthy behaviors, or even just follow their doctor's instructions.

The literature on "adherence," which used to be called "compliance," is surprising. "Adherence" means, in short, following the advice of medical experts: taking the tablets, doing the exercises, avoiding certain food stuffs, pitching up for check-ups. A surprisingly large percentage of the population simply ignore the life-saving, health-giving advice that they receive. And then they get sick, stop working and therefore paying tax, and become a burden on the state. It costs a lot of money.

It's not too difficult to do a bit of arithmetic here based on the costs of treatment. Actuaries are pretty smart at this. There is the cost of the treatment and the cost of the illness to many groups: the state, the employer, the family and the patient. So, if an unfortunate person has illness X and we know that if he or she follows a careful, but not onerous, regime the illness will have only a minimum impact on quality of life (as well as length of life), we can calculate the cost of that treatment over time. Further, if we know that when this treatment is terminated it leads to specific illness and the requirement for more and different treatments (hospitalization, operations, retirement), we can do some more arithmetic.

Now, assuming that for whatever non-rational reasons many people refuse to follow that treatment regime, we can calculate (on average) the cost to the state. So, would it not be data and money rational to pay people to follow the regime? It can be demonstrated to save money.

The same is true of other "nasty habits." Would it make sense to put all the health education money from advertisements and warnings that really don't seem to work into paying people to stop smoking, or whatever?

"What?," one hears the cry of the morally indignant puritan; "The state pay people to give up their self-inflicted addiction?" "Yes, because it makes economic sense," reply the data-literate rationalists.

The academics have been busy looking at this issue. There are plenty of papers to choose from. Does rewarding behavioral change and compliance work over the long term? Naturally, there are many complicated issues: are people who volunteer to take part in studies different from non-volunteers; for how long do they keep at it; how much to be paid; how and to whom is the money paid? And, inevitably, we have to use that mealy-mouthed word *equivocal*. That is, some results show it works and is proven to be cost efficient ... and some do not (though they are not always strictly comparable).

So, is this any more than a form of medical performance-related pay? Money, the theory goes, is a powerful, generalized re-enforcer. People do things for money ... which they can use to do precisely what they like.

Why not take this principle a little further at work. We are used to no-claims bonuses in the insurance business. So, how about paying people extra for non-absence? Money isn't docked for (real, genuine) absence, but you get a bonus if you don't take it. Perhaps there could be the same approach to accidents in this litigious society. Some jobs seem to require more safety than others.

And so it could go on. Pay people for being on time. Is this any different from the sacred overtime principle? It is all about linking pay to behavior.

Consider pay for presentism. Absenteeism costs a great deal. It is a chronic problem in some (public) sectors. Indeed, applicants' referees are often asked to comment on their referant's absenteeism record. So, work out the cost of absenteeism – extra staff having to be hired, loss of productivity, and so on – and find an economic incentive to reduce it.

Remember the line. *You are not losing pay for being absent; you are gaining pay for being present.* But imaging the outcry and the headline "taxing the sick" or "the cost of a sickie" or "struggling to work" with flu. Would those more prone to absenteeism, such as mothers of small children, kick up a great fuss? Would everyone – unions, press, customers – be noisily against it?

But perhaps this economic approach is taken already, yet in a more covert way. The public sector is quite rightly seriously concerned with absenteeism. It is discussed at selection boards. It is recorded. And it may be those with "excessive" absence (the mean is about eight days per year) don't "get on" at work quite as fast or as high as those who are not absence prone. Survival of the fittest in another form?

36 IQ testing at work

Most people on training courses experience personality tests of various sorts. Some rather enjoy them; others are skeptical about their usefulness. Old hands have been MBTI-ed to death, whilst some trainers favor more fashionable measures such as emotional intelligence. They are meant to help self-awareness and give psychological insights into "personality clashes." Bit of harmless fun, perhaps?

By and large, there is little resistance on the part of either trainers or trainees to participating in personality tests. The matter, however, becomes a little more interesting if personality tests are proposed for selection processes. Then the serious questions are asked about test reliability and validity. Selectors become nervous about rejected candidates going to lawyers or journalists to rubbish the whole procedure. So best avoided then, despite proven usefulness and efficiency?

But, if you really want a controversy, propose using *ability tests*. Personality tests are preference tests, and we are reassured that whatever your results, you're OK. But ability tests are power tests: there are right and wrong answers. It is quite difficult to see any advantages being short-changed, dim, or a few pixels short of a wide-screen. It's simply not OK to score low. There is nothing sexy about being low-wattage.

Academic psychologists who read the literature know that life is an ability test. We have data to show that brighter people live longer, make more money over their life span, and have more stable lives. And intelligence is very stable over the life-time. Measure a child at 10 and you can make good predictions about their scores at 80.

About 10 years ago, 50 of the world's top psychologists working in the area got together to explain very clearly what was known about the topic. They hammered out a creed that all agreed and signed up for. They did this in the face of various very controversial books, such as *The Bell Curve* (Herrnstein and Murray, 1994). They devised a 25-point – this is what we know – manifesto for those interested in the *science of intelligence*.

Here are parts of five of those 25 points (*Intelligence*, 2997, 24, 13–23):

A Intelligence, so defined, can be measured, and intelligence tests measure it well. They are among the most accurate (in technical terms, reliable and valid) of all psychological tests and assessments …

B Whilst there are different types of intelligence tests, they all measure the same intelligence …

C IQ is strongly related, probably more so than any other single measured human trait, to many important educational, occupational, economic and social outcomes. Its relation to welfare and performance of individuals is very strong in some arenas in life (education, military training), moderate but robust in others (social competence), and modest but consistent in others (law-abidingness) …

D A high IQ is an advantage in life because virtually all activities require some reasoning and decision-making. Conversely, a low IQ is often a disadvantage, especially in disorganized environments … There are many exceptions, but the odds for success in our society greatly favor individuals with higher IQs.

E The practical advantages of having a higher IQ increase as life settings become more complex (novel, ambiguous, changing, unpredictable or multifaceted). For example, a high IQ is generally necessary to perform well in highly complex or fluid jobs (the professions, management); it is a considerable advantage in moderately complex jobs (crafts, clerical and police work); but it provides less advantage in settings that require only routine decision-making or simple problem-solving (unskilled work).

We know that IQ is linked to job success between and within job families. It is easy to measure reliably. So what is all the fuss about? Why does every employer not use them, particularly for more senior jobs?

Those favorable to the idea of using cognitive ability/intelligence tests at work in assessment, promotion and selection note that test scores are the best single predictor of job performance (efficiency, productivity, profit). Those against such tests stress racial/ethnic minority discrimination, inequity and unfairness. These differences represent a severe, and perhaps irreconcilable, clash of values.

Yet, there remains a powerful quandary: if you emphasize and believe in efficiency and productivity criteria, and are willing to live with adverse impact, your choice is easy – use cognitive ability tests. If you emphasize equity criteria and are willing to live with lower levels of performance, longer training and more errors, your choice is also easy – remove cognitive tests and other selection devices that have strong ability components. But most business people care about *both* efficiency and equity, *both* profitability and fairness, and therefore face an interesting and complex dilemma. It's a trade-off.

One solution is to try to find non-cognitive, non-discriminatory tests that predict work performance. But more common are attempts at *distorting the evidence*. It is not unusual to hear people trot out statements about tests that have been discredited for 50 years. Worthless, disproven mantras like old slogans from failed campaigns. Few have read any serious report on the topic, but are nonetheless desperate to justify their position. Perhaps all the excitement surrounding cognitive neuropsychology and brain science will help educate people in the fundamentals of human differences in abilities.

37   Is management getting harder?

Every generation seems to believe that it is uniquely stressed or pressured at work. Everyone appears to argue that things are much tougher for them than they were for their parents or grandparents. This, despite the data showing that we work fewer hours, for much better pay, under much safer conditions and with innumerable fringe benefits.

But the stress industry, perhaps egged on by the litigation industry, is trying to persuade us otherwise. We are stressed-out slaves of horrid, demanding bosses who don't care a monkey's! Or else we have to employ fickle, feckless, unmotivated young people.

We are told, and many believe, that we are uniquely challenged by at least five factors:

The increased pace of life: everything changes more quickly than ever before. Nothing is safe, stable or likely to go unchallenged. Change comes from governments, competitors, customer demands. Change is thought of as good: listen to the way politicians use the word: a better concept is progress ... they are not the same thing.

The impact of new technology: this is in large part responsible for the increased pace of life. Technology makes people and processes redundant, but can make us too dependent on it. Think of redundant technology – film, video-tape. As those over 40 know only too well, by the time you have mastered a technology it has become obsolete.

Heightened expectations of employees and customers: want everything NOW at low prices. Employees expect total loyalty from management without showing it themselves, and seem to have unreasonable assumptions about pay and promotion. This is the cost of marketing programs about "delighting customers," perhaps. But, at the same time, so many seem unrealistic, naïve and demanding.

The loss of "deference": from all sectors of the community, making all management decisions challenged, disputed, disagreed with. The young

seem bolshy, iconoclastic and rude. They respect no one and no institutions, making them particularly difficult to manage.

Workforce diversity: it is impossible to assume that people share basic
values, and nearly everything has to be discussed and negotiated. Jokes
are forbidden: people take the slightest offence and demand humiliating
apologies.

We like to think of the 1950s as a quiet time in the workplace. People
did what was asked of them. Customers were grateful; staff respectful.
To some, even the gloomy 1970s look, retrospectively, strangely calm.
We forget all the trade union activity, the economic collapse and the four-
day week. Everything seems to have speeded up ... or has it? History tells
another story. Even the news broadcasts show how unstable past eras were,
how hard people worked and how disrespectful they often were.

And are those saviors of tomorrow, the young people who will have to
pay for the retirement luxury of their elders, different from young people
in the past? Do young people know what employers want of them? The
answer seems to be "yes." They know they need to be able to work as a
team, be self-motivated, be reliable and trustworthy, be willing to learn,
have appropriate work experience, and have both basic literacy and basic
numeracy.

But there are two very distinct and very different attitudes to young
people. Many groups, including economists, are very *positive*, predict-
ing a dramatic increase in productivity for the reasons that young people
today:

- Have higher levels of self-confidence.
- Are well-educated and comfortable with technology.
- Accept multi-culturalism, are open-minded and tolerant.
- Have global worldviews.
- Are connected 24 hours a day every day.
- Are proactive and willing to "get involved".
- Are sensitive to, and willing to fight for, social justice in the workplace.

Those positive about young people are optimistic about them and their
future. They see them as an asset that makes life better and easier. On the

other hand, some see many young workers *negatively*. They are believed to be:

- More cynical about bosses and business.
- Alienated from many aspects of the wider society, work colleagues, and so on.
- Less motivated to go to work and to do good work whilst there.
- More prone to psychological illness.
- Less respectful towards the institutions of society and office-holders in them, from courts to churches and from schools to the police.

Clearly, they are a real headache for managers. Yet, young people are obviously not a homogeneous group. Neither is the type of job that they seek or, indeed, succeed in getting.

Certainly, we do manage differently now than in the past. There are laws and procedures that attempt to protect managers and staff from each other. This certainly has made things more difficult for the tyrannical, abusive and exploitative boss. Technology has changed the speed and type of communication we have at work and has made it much easier to contact people.

So, are those who argue that management has never been so difficult correct? Is everything becoming significantly more problematic? But surely this is little more than the arrogance of modernity. What evidence is there that we, now, meet unique, unprecedented (and almost insurmountable) challenges?

Read reports from the 1950s, 1920s and 1890s and you will see that everyone believed much of the above then. Perhaps it's like the moral panic about delinquency, falling standards and the breakdown of society: a matter of great concern … to the Ancient Greeks.

38 Life after lay-off

Counselors used to remind people that it's jobs, not people, that are made redundant. "Surplus to requirements, let go, early retirement, right-sizing": all euphemisms for "involuntary unemployment."

And with it all, the well-known consequent emotions: shock and disbelief, anxiety and moodiness, gloom and depression, anger and frustration. Some people know (or, at least, believe) that, given their age, skills and experience, they will never really be fully-employed ever again.

Boom and bust come in cycles. There were many lay-offs in the early 1980s, and then again in the early 1990s. So, some 50-somethings have seen it all before. But does experience help? Having been through it myself, it was all that. Know what happens?

The road from lay-off to getting a life seems to follow various stages. The first crucial issue is the perception of procedural fairness or justice when being laid off.

Most of us know and accept the brutal facts about lay-offs. Downturn means fewer customers, less cash flow, business collapse. Companies have to right-size, otherwise they capsize.

But the question is essentially twofold: who is "fingered for the chop," and how is the process handled? Sometimes, but not often, it's pretty obvious who first deserved the yellow card. Poor performers first? Easier for managers to close a whole department or a whole section. How reasonable, rational and fearful that is perceived to be by hopefully a rational and reasonable workforce is part of the question.

The other issue is how they are let go. These range from "the key-card does not work" and "you have three hours to clear your desk" to a highly sensitive, counseling-oriented set of interviews with various experts, and then being let go with dignity.

Lay-offs are painful. Amen. Some bosses reduce their pain by increasing the pain of others. They believe the quick, surgical cut works best. That may be true of highly-skilled doctors in well-supported operating theatres. It is much less true at work.

Lay-offs lead to two problems: affective or emotional, and cognitive or thinking. Some of those laid off genuinely experience all the symptoms of post-traumatic stress disorder. They experience anxiety and depression. Some can't stop thinking about it; others can't bear to face the reality. They become withdrawn and soon fall into the vicious cycle of decline. Depression leads to withdrawal and low self-esteem, which leads to fewer attempts to find a new job or adjust, which leads to further depression.

It does not have to be like that. Some see threats as opportunities. Their appraisal is that maybe the redundancy money will give them a real opportunity to do what they really want to do. Change is embraced. It can even be heaven sent.

We are people of the heart and people of the head. How we think affects how we feel, and vice versa. Humiliate people and they get vengeful. Frighten or anger them and they get depressed. Let them go with respect and a sense of fairness, and they should soon recover.

Once laid off, you are unemployed or perhaps under-employed. Some people are offered the option of staying on with a pay cut; or going part-time; or being demoted. Some feel they do more for less; others, that the skills are not used.

Interestingly, under-employment – the idea that the job is somehow deficient to the worker – is often rather subjective. There is evidence of what is called "relative deprivation," which is all about the chasm between a person's actual and desired work situation. Most laid off workers want another (good) job. They want re-employment. A return to normality, equilibrium and respect.

What studies have shown is that post-lay-off reactions strongly influence re-employment experiences (*Journal of Organizational Behavior*, 29, 6). Whether one not only gets a job, but is also happy in it and committed to it is often a function of the lay-off experience.

Cynics may point to some personality flaw here. Negative neurotics react badly to everything, especially lay-offs, and carry their gloom and anxiety with them into the next job. Or, just as likely, insightful bosses tend not to select neurotics.

Others point to the fact that nearly everyone who loses their job needs help and support. A wise manager knows he can limit a great deal of the post-traumatic stuff like litigation, whistle-blowing and the like by ensuring the let-go processes and procedures are seen as fair.

39 Managerial educability

Management education is big business. Organizations need business-educated and business-savvy people. Managers expected to be trained, educated and up-skilled for senior jobs. Many seek out education (rather than training). The sexy letters "MBA" mean better chances of promotion and more cash.

But does an organization, in any real sense, achieve a return on their investment? Nearly all forms of education are expensive, in terms of time and money.

What is education for? Self-awareness, job satisfaction, deeper understanding or what? Surely, it is ultimately aimed at productivity? According to a shareholder perspective, the aim should be to make the company more successful as a result of better-informed, more versatile, more perceptive staff. Education must be seen to be worth it. Or, it could simply be seen as a perk to improve morale – which may, or may not, be related to any outputs.

The grey men of the bottom line want, most of all, to question how to measure learning success. And this simple question is fraught with problems. Is it enough to measure responses to the course-evaluation happy sheets, or whether the trainees' boss or colleagues or subordinates notice any difference?

But those who agonize over these well-trodden paths and well-ploughed academic fields all miss something more fundamental. Not all managers at all levels are equally *educable*.

Clearly, people differ – not only in what they take away from courses or training, but also in their skills. Why do some learn more than others? What makes one person "epistemologically hungry" and others rather bored by all these "academic questions?" Why do some thrive and others stall?

Five factors relate to all but, in particular, to managerial educability:

Intelligence: Call it "capacity" or "smarts" or "the size of your engine." Brighter people learn more quickly and more easily. They often have better recall. They go faster and further than their slower colleagues, and absorb and retain more. Most know, from school experience, where they stand on

116

the bell curve, and their "pick-up" and retention rate. Education is wasted on those a few pixels short of a wide-screen. This is about problem-solving, about being data-based and logical. It is about making good inferences. It is about testing and moderating hypotheses. Paradoxically, the more talented benefit more from training, thereby widening the gap between them and the less able.

Self-discipline: to learn well takes self-control. It requires focus and concentration, as well as giving up a range of less productive, even if more fun, activities. Learning can be hard work. The conscientious inherit the earth. Impulsive, distractible hedonists don't succeed. Education takes commitment. It means taking the long view and postponing gratification.

Self-confidence: much adult learning is about self-awareness. Self-confident people are better with criticism and negative feedback. Usually, they have something to be confident about. They recover from failures, mistakes and errors. Less confident people are less resilient, more eager to blame others rather than change or learn. They tend to be too defensive. But the self-confidence needs to be properly anchored in reality. The deluded with misplaced self-confidence in a non-existent talent are a real nightmare. In this sense, self-confidence and self-awareness are closely linked.

Perceptiveness: call it "intuition," "psychological mindedness," the "third eye." The "Aha!" experience can be exhilarating. Perceptive people have insight. It's most useful in learning about other people: what motivates them, what makes them tick. They see patterns and trends before others. They pick up on the mood of individuals and groups, and even the market.

Curiosity: Some people are simply more interested than others in "where the wires go": how things tick. This is the drive to know, to understand and to comprehend. The curious are, by definition, hungry to learn because it satisfies their curiosity. But this does not mean it soon reduces. On the contrary, training feeds it but changes the questions.

Clinicians and coaches will tell you two things, both of which should be self-evident. *First*, some people are easier to coach than others. And, *second*, sadly and paradoxically, those who need coaching the most benefit from it least. So, this is curability rather than educability, but it amounts to much the same thing. Some people are more educable than others.

There are other really important lessons that work psychologists and coaches can learn from clinical researchers. *First*, radically different types of therapy (training) appear to be equally good or bad at helping people. The main issue is whether they want to change. Self-evidently and obviously, people need to want to be trained or educated. One volunteer is worth ten conscripts. Those who go on courses determined to get something out of them, do. And those who don't, do not. Amen.

Second, the clinicians recommend that the therapy/training is preceded by some sort of assessment of what the client wants to learn and their confidence in doing so. If you don't know where you are going, any road or no road will take you there.

Management training is about learning skills (how) and obtaining knowledge (what). They should be clear as to *why* they are there, and *what* and *how* they can attain their knowledge. And what that knowledge is really for. Not just a piece of paper and letters after your name (the fallacy of credentialism) but a mindset to resolve problems, innovate and thrive.

Some managers just "get it" because they "want it" and they have the pre-requisites to gain it. The paradox is, of course, that those who need it most benefit from it least, and vice versa. That is why, so often, training does not "work." In the end, a poor investment.

40 Managerial in-experience

Here's a hypothetical question: you are asked to vote for a new CEO. There are two final candidates and they are surprisingly similar. They have near identical educational qualifications, personality traits and values. They seem equally bright. But one is aged 35 and the other is 63. Who would you choose: the dynamism and energy of youth, or the understanding and wisdom of maturity?

Most CEOs are between these hypothetical ages, usually between five and eight years either side of 50. So, what is the essential difference? The answer is that very woolly concept called *experience*. Age is "seen it all before;" "tried and tested;"; "all in good time." Youth is "do keep up;" "move with the times;" "change or die."

So, when is experience useful and relevant, and when not? What happens if the world has changed? There is nothing worse, and somehow rather pathetic, than seeing the ageing leader clinging onto the strategy, processes and procedures of a previous era that clearly do not work any longer.

Experience can be a serious handicap. People have to *unlearn* lessons and technology, which may be harder than learning them in the first place. This is less true of people issues than processes. And how easy is it to train or teach older people new things?

Certainly, governments who run pension schemes want to keep us at work, particularly in old (in both senses of the word) Europe. The number of older workers is greater than ever before: nearly three times as many aged 40, 50 and 60 than one hundred years ago. And there are quite simply not enough young people at work to pay for their generous pensions.

Around half of all Germans, two thirds of Americans, and three-quarters of Swiss people aged between 55 and 65 work full-time. In 1980, there were about twice as many aged under 30 as those over 50 in the European workforce. It is predicted that figure will reverse for the year 2020.

Do employers want older workers? Or young workers older bosses? Are they slow, doddery, forgetful and computer phobic? Or are they more reliable, conscientious and good with customers? Are grey temples reassuring, or something to worry about?

Studies do show that, quite naturally, older workers hold pretty positive views about their older peers. Interestingly, the quality and quantity of contact with older workers has very positive effects on younger workers' attitudes towards them. But older supervisors are more negative of older workers than younger supervisors.

So, what are the issues? Potential loss of productivity is a concern. The evidence, however, is that if people are in reasonable health and in the right job for their temperament and values, there is no decline whatsoever in productivity up to the age of 80. What about their *lack of enthusiasm for change and innovation*? The able employee, given good continuing training, is not necessarily change averse, even in advanced years. As much depends on their personality as on their declining abilities. Some 20-year-olds are massively change averse; some 80-year-olds very game to "have a go at something new."

By and large, CEOs are bright, energetic and engaged: more so than many their age. They are sometimes called *elite survivors*. They age well intellectually. It is not the knife or hair dye: it is intellectual fitness and flexibility.

What about their declining abilities? It is true that it may be harder to teach an old dog new tricks. Word fluency, memory, reasoning, speed of reactions do decline but, for most people, only seriously noticeably after the age of 75.

Four things influence older workers' and managers' ability and productivity. *First*, their **physical and mental health**, which influence all aspects of their social functioning. *Second*, their **education and ability**. *Third*, their **motivation and attitude to work**. *Finally*, there is the **nature of the work** itself, with its peculiar and particular set of mental and physical demands.

Older people *can* bring wise judgment and social competence. Many have greater acceptance and credibility with customers, shareholders or journalists than young people. They have often built up useful and supportive networks both inside and outside the organization. Many enjoy, and have become used to, life-long learning and continuing education: "learning a little each day, makes it far easier to stay." And many are still marked by old-fashioned values of commitment and loyalty.

Teaching older people means applying what we know about adult education more carefully. Their education, under certain conditions, works best when they are taught with meaningful and familiar materials; they can self-pace their own learning; have training on a weekly basis, rather than in blocks; they practice with new materials; and they can call on special tutors and peers for help.

So, what exactly is the "older" worker or manager? When can we expect someone to peak in terms of management? We know what is true for athletes, but what about in the boardroom?

And so, to the first question. CEOs need to be bright, hard-working and emotionally stable. They need integrity and courage, and the ability to learn. Perhaps it depends on the sector – although Steve Jobs of Apple is no spring chicken, and has suffered illness to boot. Perhaps what fades in older people is the sheer hunger for success, the drive, the ambition. As Meg Whitman (former CEO of eBay) said when searching for her successor: "Everyone I know is too rich and too tired."

41   Neuro-everything

Gurus are quick to detect the flavor of the month; the business fad that solves all problems. It is, after all, their lifeline. They find it first; and pass it on to consultants who make their middle-man killing before discarding it to poor trainers. And then it slowly dies. A shelf-life of a decade, perhaps.

But past fads, like old soldiers, never really die. They are like dormant plants in the desert waiting for the rain to fall again. They can be revived. They need repackaging and labeling in the idiom of jargon of the day, but prove very serviceable.

Fads often start in the dusty, drab and sterilized world of academia. Scientists discover something of potential interest and application. A journalist picks up and popularizes the story, omitting all the complexity and over-emphasizing the applicability. This starts a media merry-go-round that does not last long.

The next step is the *airport best seller*. The author may be a guru, may be turned into a guru, or perhaps helped by a guru who sells an idea that becomes a fad and a brand. Consultants hear about it from clients who want this new wonder-process that, through some semi-mystical process, leads to increasing profits with little pain.

The fad leads to more books, courses, even odd groups that are rather cult-like and who spread the word. But fads have a shelf-life; a sell-by date. They begin to look bland, less sexy. Doubters become skeptics who become cynics who defect. It is the eye of the storm. People are waiting for and ready for the next big idea.

We have had over a decade of "blah-blah" intelligence fads. You simply put the word "intelligence" after any other word: business, networking, spiritual, financial and, hey presto, you have an idea, a book, a course. A nice little earner, thank you. So, we have had – starting with emotional intelligence – everything from political to sexual intelligence. Even the multiple intelligence adherents seem overwhelmed by these new and baffling discoveries. Intelligences are being discovered even faster than psychiatrists are discovering disorders!

But help is at hand. And now it's not a suffix but a prefix. The new idea is "neuro." And it's really sexy. High-tech, too. It's brain science that is on a par with rocket science. So, we already have neuro-marketing and neuro-leadership. It's the brain science of ....: insert any tedious business process here. Neuro-accounting; neuro-finance, neuro-engineering. Especially neuro-advertising and neuro-marketing. At last we know why half of advertising works.

In response to cognitive (thinking) neuro-science, we now have affective (emotional) neuro-science. And, as well as intra-individual, we have inter-individual neuro-science. So, if you are a social-affective neuro-scientist, you are interested in the emotional brain in interaction with others. It attempts a physical answer to the question "Why do some people upset you so much?"

The door is open for some pretty poncy titles. How about behavioral dynamic neuro-science or gerento-linguistic neuro-science (the science of forgetting names). Not sure if neuro-health and safety quite works as well yet!

The gurus and consultants are really on the ball. There are institutes of neuro-leadership and specialist disciplines called political neuro-marketing. The neuro-practitioners are the rain-makers. This is applied brain-science. Not your old-fashioned mind control. This is circuitry. This not only tells you what people are thinking, but also offers the much more exciting opportunity to shape how they are thinking.

The gurus have caught the excitement of the neuro-scientists. Neuro-science has taken off over the past decade. It is a multi-disciplinary, trillion-dollar race to understand how the brain works.

What has helped a great deal is the development of new, powerful, ever-changing measurement techniques (MRI, PET scanning). We used to examine bumps on the head; now, we watch the electricity in the brain. What "lights up" when you see an ad or try to solve a problem? What parts of the brain do people use for decision-making or flirting? Why are there differences between people?

Can we test advertisements in PET-scans? Can we choose leaders as a function of their MRI output? Sure we can: but is this wise? The scientists are excited but wary. There is much progress, but some way to go. The findings are still crude; the theories unsure; the results tentative.

But the gurus can't and won't wait for the science to catch up with their ideas. The science is the "mere-detail" stuff for the gurus. We will surely soon know when and where and why advertising works. We can do neuro-branding that gives results. Mind control is the result of understanding brain science. Ah, the holy grail of marketers and dictators. The ministry of propaganda now really becomes efficient.

The real neuro-scientists are excited but cautious. They know that many crucial issues remain unsolved. What is the neurological basis of consciousness or sleep, and of various intriguing mental illnesses such as mania or addictions?

The dilemma for the scientist is often about public education, outreach and funding. Many need large amounts of money: from public funds. If the public seem to back their enterprise, the chances of getting more money go up. But much of the public is used to a diet of tabloid science – simplistic miracle cures. So, a proportion of popular science still deals in unlikely promises of amazing breakthroughs.

The scientist and the journalist have an uneasy friendship. But neither troubles the gurus much.

42   Nice guys come second

Personality researchers have identified a dimension of personality called *agreeableness*. Agreeable people are forgiving, trusting and straightforward. They are also generous, tolerant, altruistic and warm-hearted. Modest and tender-minded, they also make loyal friends and good neighbors. To be labeled "an agreeable sort of person" is a compliment.

But they come second, often last, in business. Alas, the *disagreeable* inherit the earth and most easily climb the greasy corporate pole. Agreeableness is a business handicap.

What are they like, these disagreeable people? Suspicious and skeptical, demanding and egocentric; impatient and intolerant, self-confident and headstrong, competitive and antagonistic; assertive and argumentative. The classic definition of a bastard is "a vicious, despicable, or thoroughly disliked person."

The data are clear about successful business leaders: the *higher* you score on agreeableness, the *less* likely you are to succeed as a business leader. Pity, but there it is. The question is why.

And don't be hoodwinked by the PR guff that surrounds the modern business leader. They spend fortunes trying to look agreeable: nice to their staff, customers, shareholders, babies, and little old ladies trying to cross the street. Warm, compassionate and caring for the environment and the "little people." But those in the know, and those who matter, are clear that they are tough, bold and competitive.

Few disagreeable bastards, however, rejoice in their real personality. Clearly, the best prototype is Michael O'Leary from Ryan Air. It has been said of him that his abrasive management style, ruthless pursuit of cost-cutting, and explicitly rude and hostile attitude towards corporate competitors, airport authorities, governments, unions and customers have become a hallmark. Is he faking bad? Or rather, is he one of the few really successful business managers who is as he seems – which, in part, accounts for why he is successful?

Agreeable people are certainly more popular than disagreeable people. But agreeableness is not an asset in the boardroom, the courtroom or the battlefield. Being competitive, being critical and skeptical of others' behavior and motives works well for people in business. You have to be vigilant and alert for the tricks of your competitors. Business is about survival of the fittest: it is not a gentleman's game.

The real question is, would you prefer to work for an agreeable or disagreeable boss? The first response is definitely the nice guy: a warm, caring and sharing, straightforward individual. But if you have had this experience, you soon see why it is not a good choice.

One of the main functions of a boss is to "kick arse" when required: to confront (and rectify) poor performance. Agreeable bosses are too forgiving: they give people a second (and third and fourth) chance. They are easily manipulated by the indolent and conniving; those with many illness excuses and a deep sense of entitlement. The agreeable boss lets those people off the hook, makes special cases for people and is well-known as being a "soft touch."

The agreeable boss is too generous at appraisal. He gives "average" when "poor" or "downright unacceptable" is the right box to check. Many labor under the erroneous assumption that rewards work, rather than punishments. But, by being too kind to the under-performers, the agreeable boss causes manifold problems.

Clearly, it really and rightly upsets the good performers, who notice very little differentiation between their rewards and the ratings of those that everyone knows to be well below average. Next, the message is given to the under-performers that it is all OK: indeed, that their performance is good. So, this results in simultaneously de-motivating the good performers and making the poor performers complacent. That is the frequent result from the soft-hearted, tender-minded, sympathetic boss.

People often get angry with an agreeable boss because they seem to be easily manipulated by less agreeable staff … who eventually get their job. The agreeable boss can be erratic and unpredictable. Because of the "special circumstances" they have to deal with – as they see it – agreeable bosses seem particularly vulnerable to abuse by Machiavellian staff.

So, how can the agreeable person make it to the top? There seem to be three things they can do. *First*, **learn the scripts**. All sorts of professionals are taught how to deliver bad news (doctors, nurses, and so on). They learn the words and phrases in the right order. Many jobs are scripted: you can hear it in sales people and serving staff. The scripts help consistency and take away embarrassment. There are scripts for under-performing, demanding and absconding staff, and they can be learnt and practiced. They can be learnt on assertiveness and counseling skills training courses.

Second, **use procedures and practices**. Most organizations are flooded with internally and externally generated laws, regulations and procedures that deal with issues at work from bullying to theft, and absenteeism to incompetence. Some agreeable people feel that they can "take themselves out of the equation" by the simple application of these procedures.

Third, read the **tough love** literature. Agreeable bosses cause business failure: hardly an altruistic act. They are beaten, overtaken and sidelined by those who really understand business.

Skeptical, anatagonistic competitives win the race. They get to the top of the tree and have the stomach for the fight. Some feign a spot of agree-ableness for the cameras, but others don't bother.

43   The normality of silos

What have management gurus got against grain farmers? They complain of the evils of silo thinking and silo mentality, and want silo destruction. Silos are bad, matrices are good!

Visitors to the fly-over mid-west states are often impressed by those magnificent gatherers of the harvest. Suddenly a mini-Manhattan of sky scrapers appears on the horizon. Canary Wharf on the prairie.

The silo metaphor is all about lack of interconnections, like those blocks of flats in Dubai or bank headquarters in the City. They are *stand-alones*, not linked to other buildings. In organizational terms, what this means is poor communication, own agendas, lack of synergy.

A silo is the enemy of centralism, but also of managerialism. Silos tend, over time, to do things their own way, develop their own micro-climate, pursue their own goals. And they do so happily, perhaps even healthily.

Further, the silo is also the enemy of heterogeneity, and this, perhaps, is its greatest "fault." People in silos are alike and think alike and, as a result actually, like each other. They see the world in the same way. And they like it like that. The same grain from the same harvest.

How natural are silos? Why do people of similar type and function seem to congregate together? What's the pull? The answer lies in abilities, personality, values and socialization.

Vocational guidance is about putting round pegs in round holes. It is about "fit." The right person for the right job. Why does a young person choose to become an engineer or a salesperson? Why a police person or a shop owner? Yes, Fate plays a part. People "inherit" businesses, but they also inherit skills and abilities. Some are born into wealth; others, poverty. Some get a "leg-up;" others have to claw their way to the top.

Many people find out what they are good at along the way. They discover their abilities, strengths or talents. These may be (in the language of school subjects) in mathematics, or English, science or arts. They may discover their real strengths. Some are good at technology and things; others at "the people stuff." Some have a high IQ; others, a high emotional quotient. Some are divergent thinkers; others, convergent thinkers.

Some are extroverts attracted to jobs with variety, stimulation and a great deal of people contact. Others find all that rather too over-stimulating and prefer a quieter life. Some prefer face-to-face contact; others, email. Some get stressed by disorder and chaos; others live their life that way. Some yearn for power; others, achievement.

There are many ways to differentiate between people and jobs. Those interested in people vs. those interested in tasks/objectives; those with divergent vs. convergent thinking; those who are "left-" rather than "right-brained." People of similar persuasion tend to make similar educational – and thence job – choices, and end up working with one another.

This is how silos form. Consider the marketing (and sales) vs. the finance silo. Quite early on, some people discover they like, are interested in or are good at marketing. They learn – often, very early on at school – that they are "persuasive." They work on their talents, become interested in the area and may choose to study the subject in further education.

The same is true of finance people, who usually have a facility with math and arithmetic. They often enjoy mind puzzles like Sudoku and see patterns easily. They frequently study the subject later.

People are selected for their appropriateness to a vacancy by people in the silo. Selectors look for a "good fit" – a type, a skill and attitude set. Often, whether they admit it or not, they tend to choose people like themselves.

And then they start the process of socialization or introduction into the corporate subculture. They are taught how to see the world, what the current issues are, what the major problems are and how to solve them.

People who are "not quite right;" who don't fit the mold; who feel the job is not really for them, leave. Hardly pearls discharged by oysters but, rather, those who choose to find something that fits them better. So, those who stay become more alike.

It is a truism, but also true, that there are accounting types or marketing types. Crude, disparaging, stereotypes do have a kernel of truth about them … otherwise the jokes would not be funny. And people who work together are usually placed physically side-by-side at work – sometimes in different buildings, or at least on different floors of the same building.

But are silos bad things? Only if the people in them don't realize they are all working for the same organization. And only if they see the occupiers of other silos as the enemy. The old Japanese model was for young people to understand the business fully by working in different sections to start off with and being moved frequently. This, they believed, gave the young a good sense of how the organization worked. They had a broad picture, not a narrow one, to take with them as they ascended the corporate ladder. They jumped from silo to silo in a sort of matrix way. A good solution? Maybe not, if the Japanese economy over the past 15 years is anything to go by.

44 The off-site strategy meeting

It is not uncommon for the "grown-ups" in the organization to have a "jolly" in a fine country hotel. These arrangements are more likely to be described as "the off-site board meeting," the "annual strategy weekend" or the "director's workshop."

They can take many forms. In bull markets, they may take place abroad. Partners may be invited, though they have their own, supposedly very different program. In bear markets, the five-star country hotel – out of season, hopefully with a golf course – near to headquarters must suffice.

What happens at these meetings? Why do they occur "off-site?" Can they in any way justify the high cost, whatever the market? These weekends can take many different forms, of course. Some are facilitated by consultants; some have a more playful fun-and-games aspect than others. Some have a balanced work–play agenda, whilst others involve nothing but work. So, what goes on?

There are some common themes. The aim is to analyze the business and the strategy, and to get commitment and "buy in." Some groups rely on simple but effective SWOT analyses whereby they work out where they are, and should be going. Others might try to be a little more experimental or metaphorical, perhaps being given tasks in the hotel garden or pool – "build a bridge, make a raft." Some split into small groups; alternatively, everyone stays together all the time.

Some groups rely on a coach, counselor or consultant to keep them on track or lead the discussion. Sometimes that person is a process consultant whose job it is to observe how people are relating to each other, their feelings and "leaking," rather than what they are saying about the business. They do the people dynamic, pointing out often rather uncomfortable truths about how partners/directors appear to loathe, distrust and undermine each other. Some boards prefer to get in experts, motivational speakers or minor gurus (supposedly) to help them understand the business better.

But these weekends can have common goals. They do aim to bring about a shared, agreed and practical way ahead. This involves agreeing a destination, an objective, a hoped-for bright future. This part is usually reasonably conflict-free and can help the mood go nicely upbeat. The analysis of the current situation is often less pleasing. This can turn into a blame-storming session (hence the coach) when things aren't going well. The outcome can be a realistic, detailed appraisal of "the state we are in." This, of course, leaves the gulf between the now and the future: the start and the destination. That is all about the journey, once there is agreement on the distance to be traveled.

Then come the strengths and weaknesses, force-field, opportunities–threats stuff. It's about listing, prioritizing and, again, agreeing those factors that are going to make the journey possible, even pleasant, and those that are holding back progress. This part is often the most interesting for three reasons. The *first* is, obviously, agreement on what these forces are. This can surprise, frustrate, even anger participants, as one person's strengths are another's weakness. The *second* is where to invest your energy – reinforcing the strengths or defeating the weaknesses. This is about time, effort and money. That really does wake people up. And the *third* issue is about individual roles in all of this.

And it is the latter point that partly explains the "off-site luxury hotel" approach. Whilst the ideal picture of the board of directors or partners is one of a harmonious, talented group pulling together and pooling their resources for the betterment of the organization, the reality is often very different. The partners will often be competitive, egocentric and ambitious people, looking out primarily for Number 1.

Offices have territories and distractions. They have, for many people, memories and ghosts. Hotels offer neutral space, and they may have other facilities that help: the gym, the pool and the golf course. But, most of all, late night, "guards down," alcohol-fuelled conversations in the bar can be very illuminating. Powerful alpha males find personal conversation difficult, however important they may be. Booze, a good coach and silly games might help. Might.

One objective of the meetings is "understanding each other better." Perhaps, also, better self-understanding. And this partly explains the point of inviting partners/significant others along. These people play two roles: *first,* to give insight into the accompanied director/managers. The partner and the relationship can give surprising insight into their work behavior – after all, partners are the "life" part in the "work–life balance." But, *second,* partners can have powerful influences. Ask directors in a 360-degree exercise who knows them best, and many say "my partner" – and this is not said in jest. To have partners interact, and even form supportive alliances, can be extremely important. It can also backfire. Some don't have partners, others have partners of the same sex, others a rather racy track record from another generation.

So, an expensive, pointless jolly for the grown-ups, or a terribly important, psychologically crucial interaction? The off-site away days can be the most useful thing the board ever does – but their success does, not happen by chance. Some turn into cathartic booze-ups; others into mind-numbing tedium. The best, however, may represent the best training and development investment the organization ever makes.

45 On the other hand

Most of us need to assess and describe, evaluate and profile other people as part of our daily jobs. It means writing references and making people judgments. Over the years, people develop idiosyncratic theories based on their experience: that temper is associated with redheads; lack of integrity of those with beards; carelessness (or worse, wickedness) with left-handedness and narcissism with the wearing of bling. Some have a rich vocabulary with which to describe the personality and motivation of others; in some, this is surprisingly poor. Some appear insightful, psychologically-minded, astute; others, perhaps because of their interest in things rather than people, are unable to give a good "pen picture" of individuals, even those they know well. The question for psychologists, for at least the last hundred years, is how most parsimoniously and accurately to describe an individual's personality.

Investigators have adopted three methods. Over 75 years ago, one enterprising chap went through the dictionary and found around 36,000 personality-related words. But, when categorized, the number became much more manageable. This is called the *lexical* approach, and it still exists. Curiously, perhaps, whichever language you choose, you find the same groupings.

The second approach is *theory-based*. This addressed the "ancient" Greeks (i.e. Galen) or "modern" psychologists (i.e. Jung) to search for the best descriptions of people. But to say a person is phlegmatic or choleric does not seem to go down well today.

The third approach is *empirical*. This measures people on many kinds of criteria using their own assessments (i.e. questionnaires) or the judgments of others (i.e. ratings), and then subjecting them to statistical analysis, looking for underlying patterns and relationships.

The different methods sometimes yielded reasonably similar results. Thus, the theory-based approach of Melanie Klein suggested three factors similar to that of the empirically based approach of Hans Eysenck. They spoke of three dimensions: one where people went **toward** other people; another, **away from**; or a third, **against**.

The debate went on for a long time. Academics do split hairs. But, gradually, there was enough consensus for the field to progress. There seemed to be five dimensions; five continua or rating scales that were unrelated to each other and that captured the nature of the individual. Proof emerged that these dimensions were biologically-based, substantially heritable and stable over time. People can be placed at either end or somewhere in the middle. Every dimension is a bell-curve: the nearer you are to the middle, the more average and "normal" you are. And vice versa: extreme scores are rare, more unusual, less normal. And, of course, it is the less common, more extreme scores that are most interesting and memorable. But there is a catch – a trade-off. With each advantage comes a disadvantage.

To start with the best known: *introversion–extroversion*. Top jobs require the appearance of extraversion because management and leadership are contact sports. Extroverts are socially dominant, positive and assertive. They seem to make friends easily; to be good persuaders and influencers; and to have emotional intelligence. But extroverts are accident-prone. They trade off accuracy for speed – they put their foot in it. They can be easily prone to boredom and therefore unwilling to sustain the long periods of serious concentration frequently required in top jobs. They are likely to be promiscuous in every sense of the word.

The second dimension often requires some politically correct term such as "negative affectivity" or "emotional adjustment." We used to call it "neuroticism." There are nervy people: those prone to anxiety, depression, hypochondriasis. They rarely get to the top. It's all too stressful. But they are vigilant about the emotional state of others, which can be an advantage.

But what of the cool as ice, imperturbable, stable individual? Great in a crisis perhaps, yet lacking in real empathy for those who seem a little frightened, bewildered or pressured. Further, some anxiety is a good driver. It makes people prepare harder so they don't fail. It makes people more sensitive to the emotions and moods of others. It is often associated with being vigilant for problems. The highly stable individual can stumble too.

The third dimension, called **openness to experience**, is associated with creativity, a life of the mind and an interest in the aesthetic. Open people are curious, ready to have a go and try something new. Those low in this dimension are thought of as practical, grounded sorts. Creativity is linked with innovation, which is a good thing. Open people can, and want, to "think outside the box." They can, in combination with other skills, have breakthroughs. But the downside is the impractical dreamer.

Those caught up in a fantasy, *Star Wars* world of futurology as the business around them collapses. They may be seriously impractical: dreamers and time-wasters wedded to mad projects.

The fourth dimension is *agreeableness*. High-scorers are empathic, tender-minded and kind. They do the "caring and sharing" thing well. And, as a result, they are often well-liked. But, alas, not always well-respected. The downside of agreeableness at work is a reluctance to confront. The agreeable manager forgives, seeks help for others and gives them another chance. The disagreeable manager "kicks arse," threatens and sacks. They may not be liked, but they are frequently greatly respected by staff who see the agreeable manager letting colleagues "get away with murder" and never pulling their weight.

The final dimension is *conscientiousness*, prudence, the work ethic. Difficult to think of anyone getting to the top who did not have the drive for achievement, the organization and the efficiency associated with this dimension. But the workaholic is high in conscientiousness, as is the perfectionist. Some plodders have to work very hard because they are not as able as others.

So, should the ideal workers be high on extroversion and conscientiousness; low on agreeableness and neuroticism; average on openness? Well, that really depends on how extreme the scores, various other crucial abilities *and* the nature of the job.

It's a case of on the other hand: the downside to the upside, the dark to the bright side.

46   A paradox resolved

In 1973, an economist called Easterlin published a paper that has worried economists ever since. He showed, as have others, that wealth is, in effect, unrelated to happiness. Now very famous, a graph from that work has been reproduced many times. It shows, using American data, two lines over a 50-year period: the one wealth and the other happiness. Wealth goes up steadily, happiness remains flat.

The first thing to do was to replicate the finding, to see whether it was robust. It was. The same pattern was found in different countries. This puzzled and frustrated many economists because, to some extent, their discipline was predicated on there being a positive relationship between the two. To many, this meant happiness: or so they thought.

Other social scientists, however, were not surprised, as it confirmed what they had believed (and preached) all along. Various explanations were offered. The *first* was the **threshold** argument. Money does make people "happier," or at least have greater well-being, **up to a point**, but after that it has less and less "power to please." So, as nations became richer and more people reached the threshold, increasing wealth had less and less effect. This is the "enough" concept. After all, how many houses, cars, watches, televisions do you want or need? The question of greatest interest, of course, was how much is enough? At what income level does the graph start to flatten?

A *second* explanation, favored by psychologists, was that people **adapt** to increasing wealth very quickly. Its power soon fades. That is why money is only a good motivator in the very short term. We get used, very quickly, to good things and then expect to receive them.

Third, there is the issue of social comparison. What makes people happy is not absolute but, rather, comparative wealth. Happiness occurs when you are doing better than your peers. Hence the fury at bonus time: it's all about "my great wad of cash compared with yours." This, of course, leads to the amazing conclusion that people could be made as happy by lowering the salary of everyone else as by raising theirs.

A *fourth* argument went that wealth did, indeed, make people happier, but that other contemporaneous social changes cancelled out its effect.

So, an increase in divorce and a decrease in the sense of community cancelled any well-being derived from increased wealth.

Others tried to criticize the actual measure of happiness as being too simple-minded, too uni-dimensional, too naïve. They argued, as indeed the data showed, happiness can be very volatile depending on the precise circumstances in which questions are answered. It has also been argued by some psychologists that happiness is essentially a personality variable. Some people are by nature happy, whilst others (even those with money enough to buy a great deal of therapy) remain gloomy. Stable extroverts are dispositionally happy: neurotic introverts the reverse – however much money they have or don't have.

But there has been another take on the problem. American sociologist Claude Fischer (2008) replicated the money/happiness relationship. He plotted happiness and GDP from 1972 to 2005. He found GDP nearly doubled, whilst happiness was stable – perhaps showing a small decline. So, once again, the paradox.

However, he argued that it is a very poor index of the general population's material well-being, because income is heavily skewed. Left-wing people have always made much of the very uneven distribution of wealth. We used to hear the ratio 7:84 bandied about: 7 percent of the British population owned 84 percent of the wealth. In some countries, the income differential between baker and banker, the waiter and the waited upon is incredibly large; in others quite small.

What, our intrepid researcher asked, if he used median household income, or, indeed, median male income? Plot that and things look very different. The former was 1.2 times and the latter only 1.1 times greater in 2003–05 compared with 1972–74. In other words, if you plot a different measure of wealth, it takes out the skew and the graphs become very similar.

The next explanation was that people were getting richer because (primarily) they were working harder. Breadwinners worked longer; partners tended to work more. Time was lost in commuting, working on the Blackberry and the additional money earned simply went into child care. So, the net material gain was lost.

Then again, by plotting wealth by gender-neutral hourly wages, the two graphs begin to look identical. Use that as a measure of wealth and it looks relatively closely linked to happiness.

So, the paradox is resolved: the increased wealth of the average person has been bought at the cost of well-being. Economists can rest easily. So can theologians. Pursuing wealth can cost too much. Best inherit it … but that's another story.

47 The personality of interviewers

To what extent does the personality of the *interviewer* play a significant role in the whole interview process? Do *different* types make *different* decisions on the *same* people given the *same* criteria? This phenomenon is observable in group interviews, where members of a panel together interview a candidate.

Consider how introverted and extroverted interviewers approach the task, and what they look for. Extroverts usually enjoy interviewing. They are "people people;" sociable; eager to be amused and entertained. Extroverts probably talk too much and listen too little. They may not do their preparation as thoroughly as they should. They may be impatient and inattentive in long interviews. They may be attracted to vivacious (if vacuous) candidates.

Introverts pause more, seeming hesitant, when they are processing information. They can find the whole process tiring and intimidating, and feel more for those candidates who are similar to themselves. They usually take the data gathering more seriously, and see the whole interview less as a social occasion than as a semi-scientific exercise. Introverted candidates probably get a "better deal" (more favorable hearing) from the introverted interviewer. The trouble is that introverts eschew interviewing assignments, whilst extroverts volunteer for them. The world, it seems, favors the extrovert.

And what of the "sensitive," unstable, low adjustment (neurotic) interviewer? They are the fragile flowers of the world, often hypersensitive to real and imaginary threats. They are stress-prone and don't like people in general, whom they see as threatening. They can be bitchy and critical; wary and judgmental. Paradoxically, many are attracted to being counselors, though many need counseling themselves.

Neurotic interviewers can easily feel threatened by the potential "mover and shaker." They worry about things: the future, the present; their reputation, their security; their ability, their respect-worthiness, and so on. They listen carefully to the candidates' answers to questions about work–life balance, diversity, counseling and other issues. If they don't like what they hear in response to salient as well as less relevant questions, their instinct is to push the rejection button.

Stable interviewers, like stable employees, are better news. They are less irritable and moody, and better able to weigh the information. They worry less about what might go wrong and cope with all the little dramas at interviews well. They tend to be calm, focused and rational.

Agreeable interviewers are warm, empathic and trusting. They are, for the most part, likeable. They understand that interviews can be stressful. They are concerned about making the candidate comfortable, relaxed and able to be their real selves. They are slow to chide and swift to bless.

Less agreeable, tough-minded, interviewers believe you understand people best by "putting them on the spot." They treat the interview as a "Paxman-inspired" political interview. They cross-examine individuals, often pushing them to give details of success and failure that their CV overlooks. They are hard to please: cynical and world-weary, and they care little for the interviewee's comfort.

Conscientious interviewers are not only conscientious about how they approach the task of interviewing, but also what they are looking for. Hard work is a virtue. Often, but not always, conscientiousness is associated with conservatism and a moral sense. Conscientious interviewers are concerned that the applicant follows orders, obeys rules and has a sense of duty. They admire the arrive early–stay late ethos, though this does not mean they are necessarily workaholics.

Less conscientious interviewers want to have fun. They tend to be less achievement-orientated, less careful and with a much weaker work ethic. All that "postponement of gratification" stuff never worked with them. They prefer what the Freudians call "the pleasure principle." And it shows in the interview. They seek out playmates more than solid and reliable colleagues.

What of the abilities of the interviewer? How are bright, educated interviewers different from their less-talented peers? Another paradox: the clever prefer discriminating questions; the dim prefer "clever" questions. Brighter people tend to have a bigger vocabulary and think fast. They ask good questions that sort the wheat from the chaff.

The less-bright and less well-educated interviewers might rehearse "killer" questions that make them appear intelligent, even if they cannot process the answers. They often have "crackpot" theories, refreshingly evidence-free about desirable characteristics in candidates.

The interview is a social process. It can be a sophisticated intellectual theatrical show, a hall of mirrors, a game of bluff and counter-bluff. There is no doubt that there is a lot of "gut feeling" going on in both parties, despite all their training. Hence the importance of the personality and values of the interviewers. All candidates know about the nice-and-nasty interviewer routine and clearly warm to some interviewers, rather than others.

So, the moral of the story? *First*, acknowledge that the interviewer's make-up (ability and personality) do inevitably play a part. *Second*, try to work out how specific interviewers react to particular candidates. *Third*, use multiple interviewers, but particularly those with the ability and personality profiles found among those actually doing the job in question. *Fourth*, where possible, encourage these insights in interviewers. *Fifth*, choose (yes, and train) interviewers who are bright, stable and conscientious.

48 Political skills

Forget all that competency nonsense about "helicopter-view" and team work, emotional intelligence and integrity. The greatest asset you have in business is political skill: discuss.

It is obvious, once you consider the rather clumsy definition: *the ability to understand others effectively at work and to use such knowledge to influence others to act in ways that enhance one's personal and/or organizational objectives.* Not quite the same as being influential; not as ruthless as Machiavellianism. And not as mushy as emotional intelligence.

You can be bright, hardworking and emotionally intelligent but, unless you have political skill, you will be an "also ran." It is a skill that not only helps you get *along with* people, but also get *ahead of* them. Sure, it's a soft skill, a people skill, but it does have recognizable components. What are they?

Social astuteness: this is about being perceptive, insightful, attuned to all the vagaries and nuances of everyday interactions. It is about being psychologically-minded. Picking up the clues and cues. Reading between the lines; the subtexts. Seeing the meaning in things. Aware of self and others: how you are "coming across;" what they are really saying. Understanding the motives of others through the disguises.

Interpersonal influence: this is about being persuasive in different contexts. It inevitably means being adaptable and flexible. Bi-or tri-lingual in the languages of persuasion – visual, vocal, verbal. It is about monitoring self and others sufficiently to be able to charm, cajole and persuade. And it's about knowing about, and practicing, those famous (Robert Cialdini's) six and only six influencing principles: recriprocity, commitment and consistency, social proof, authority, liking, and scarcity.

Networking ability: this is about more than having a good address book or being vivacious at dinner parties. It is understanding the usefulness of – and, more importantly, being able to establish – a range of alliances, coalitions and friendship networks. This involves the serious skills of deal-making, conflict management and negotiation. They can be assets that need to be established and then "tapped" from time to time. They "come in handy" at different times and for different reasons.

Apparent sincerity: ah yes, that great oxymoron. It is about being able to look authentic and genuine on all occasions, irrespective of what you really think or feel. Call it "emotional labor" or "good acting," it is the ability not to show coerciveness, manipulativeness, or that one has ulterior motives. What you see is not what you get. Sincerity is showmanship: its good acting and really understanding emotions.

It's perfectly obvious why political skill is the king of skills at work. It builds social and political capital. Employees like to have a boss with this skill. It does them good: if, of course, he or she uses that skill to further the success of the team as a whole, not only themselves. And senior leaders like it in their staff.

But go back to the definition. It is all in the idea that political skill can enhance personal *and/or* organizational objectives. Fine, if they are aligned; a bit of a problem if they are not. What if political skills are used against the organization, or even just against colleagues trying to climb the greasy pole?

Perhaps this is why the concept suggests politics at work has such a negative association. Being political suggests being devious, underhand, sly … possibly even corrupt. Yet, it is a critical factor in managerial effectiveness. Being political and exercising political skills are not the same thing. Political skill is about understanding the people side of business. It is all about good interaction with key people and about maintaining visibility.

Consider the skills of very successful politicians, whether you like them or not. Blair and Clinton: ask people who know them and they talk of charm, charisma, confidence. They talk about being "won over" and of feeling special in their company. They talk of (apparent) honesty and sincerity. And those who were less successful? Bush and Brown, for instance. Yes, they became leader of their party and the country. That takes some skill. But what of their soft skills?

Political skills are essential for getting noticed and for building a reputation. They are central to getting along with people at work, both managing up and managing down. Again, go back to the definition: what is somebody like who is not socially astute? Gauche? A nerd/techie? What is someone like who cannot persuade, charm and influence? Do they ever make it to the first hurdle?

The really interesting question is how, when and where you can acquire, increase or polish up this skill. There do not seem to be many courses called "Acquiring Political Skills." And even if there were, what would they be like? How much of this stuff can you really teach?

Some time ago, it was claimed that CEO skills are first observed and learnt in the school playground. Political skills, as defined in this essay, are very useful at all stages of life, particularly in the tough world of school of bullies and gangs. Children know how important it is to be "cool," to be accepted by the top gang. Getting in, and staying in, is a political skill.

And maybe, if you have not worked that out or picked it up by the time you get to work, you never will.

49 Process, profit and people

Go through a good MBA class and ask people about their background. Yes, there will be a number of oddballs: priests and doctors, actors and architects; but these classes are usually dominated by two groups of people – engineers and accountants.

The situation with engineers is so serious in some countries that governments are becoming seriously worried. Supply never meets demands because soon after qualification – and, where necessary, paying back their loan, off they go to business school to become rich, successful, captains of industry.

It's easier to explain accountants: they want to widen their perspective; understand the whole business. Accounts give one a very profound idea of how businesses run: profit and loss and all that, but there is a wider picture.

By definition, accountants and engineers have a facility with numbers. They see patterns, do calculations, apply formulae with ease! They often stride through what are considered to be the hardest parts of the course – that is, finance, econometric modeling, some parts of strategy. They are convinced, and partly rightly, that everything lies in the numbers.

Engineers understand business processes. They understand how to design systems that lead to efficiency. They know about the necessity of integrating the moving parts. They know how technology can radically alter how things are done, and they appreciate flow models: hence the fashion a few years ago for process-re-engineering. It seemed to imply that structural issues were of major importance. Critiqued later as a quick-fix, short-term move, that simply took out middle management and derailed the company, it enjoyed wide-spread success.

The eye of the engineer, their understanding of how things fit together and operate can be a great asset in business. It is no wonder that the great production line time-and-motion people were engineers by training.

Accountants often have the best understanding of the health of a business. This is more than reading or drawing up a profit and loss statement. Often, they understand *real* costs, and have a good eye for real waste and savings. They also, very usefully, come to know legal issues surrounding tax. They can save companies fortunes by recommending changes that have high tax implications. The best have a good knowledge of finance, stock markets and currency speculation. More than most, they understand global monetary issues and trends.

Both accountants and engineers take to strategy. Indeed, many leave business school to join the great management consultancy firms which often describe themselves as strategy consultants. They offer a careful (in-depth, brilliant, total) analysis of the current state of the organization and, as a result, recommendations of what should be done.

Go through the presentation pack and see the work and thinking of accountants and engineers. It comes (relatively) easily to them. And it's beguiling for the less well-trained. Closely argued and supported by mountains of data and analysis, these "outsiders" appear to understand one's own organizations far better than "insiders" who have worked there for a decade.

But there appears to be something missing in all this: people. When managers are young, they believe the problems lie in structures or strategy; processes or products but, as they get older, its people. Get a dozen CEOs of small businesses (those with a turnover of $50 million or less) and ask them to list their major (ongoing, intransigent) problems. Sure, they may mention bank loans or leases on buildings but, more often, it's about individuals. They are less interested in how people tick, as opposed to how to solve the problem of particular individuals who are "difficult."

People-people are often not particularly interested in business. Of course, this begs the question as to who they are. Certainly, anthropology or psychology degrees guarantee nothing about people skills. Study great novels, if you want to really understand the vicissitudes of human behavior. It may be argued that those arts graduates who read great literature receive a far better insight into the foibles, peccadilloes and capricious behavior of people.

In business, those (supposedly) most interested in people issues and welfare are those in human resources (HR). HR has changed over time, as has the label they have given themselves. Originally simply called the Staff Department, many now call themselves the Talent Management Department or, even more simply, the People Department. HR departments deal with many issues, like pay-roll, industrial relations, health and safety, and so on.

If the accountants and the engineers look after the other resources (finance, plant, stock, knowledge), the HR department looks after the human side of things. Yet, comparatively few HR directors sit on the board, and few CEOs come from an HR background. Further, HR is almost universally disliked and reviled: thought to be a waste of money.

Perhaps, too often, HR cannot help the senior managers with the real people issues. Perhaps they do not have the skills or the courage to do so. Perhaps people problems are amongst the most intractable of all problems. Perhaps they have tried to "ape" the engineers, have become too obsessed by processes and procedures, and have forgotten what they are really trying to do. It is the people-oriented, psychologically-minded, emotionally literate accountant/engineers that seem to do best.

50　Reassuringly expensive

What is the relationship between the price of a business coach and the outcome of the coaching? Why do the prices of coaches differ so dramatically? What factors come into play when coaches decide how much to charge a potential client?

Therapists say money is important in therapy. They talk of a *reasonable sacrifice*; of a symbol of patient effort; of valuing what they are getting. Some relate that patients withhold payment when they are angry with their therapist; or make various interesting "slips of the pen" when writing payment checks (unsigned, incorrect amount, misfit between words and numbers; misspelling the therapist's name).

Most executives don't pay for their own coaching. It's part of their personal development. But how do those who purchase the service know whether they are getting value for money? In short, how do you go about selecting a coach who can "do the business" – if, indeed, you even know what that actually is?

There are manifold criteria that might be employed in choosing a coach:

- Does the coach have accredited, formal, independent *training* (some real qualifications)?
- Does the coach have enough and appropriate *business experience* and experience of coaching?
- Does the *chemistry* work (are the two parties involved matched in energy, humor, politics, world-view)?
- Does the coach have a coherent theory/framework/model that he or she can explain clearly and intelligibly?
- How does the coach propose to *measure* the outcome (what, when and why)?
- Is the coach being *supervised* by another more senior/experienced person?
- How *self-aware* does the coach appear to be?
- What is the coach's *contracting* process?

You could go on reputation and price: if they come well recommended and charge a great deal, surely that is enough. Is it good to be reassuringly expensive? Perhaps hairdressers are a fair comparison: what is the relationship between the price of a visit and the outcome?

But perhaps we need first to know how the process works, and to obtain the answers to some fundamental questions:

What is the average cost of a coaching session for a senior manager today?

The answer is a great range, with a bi-modal, double-peak, cheap-and-cheerful vs. reassuringly expensive and smug group. The first are in the $150–$4000 range; the others $750–$1,500 range, **per hour**. Obviously, independents can be a great deal more flexible about the fee. Some lower the fee if the job looks particularly interesting, or if they think it might get them into a particular organization. They may have to charge less, if the coaching is just part of a larger program.

And a typical contract: $15K for a six-month program to include some initial psychometric assessment, telephone or face-to-face interviews with a half a dozen people who know the client, the sessions themselves (perhaps two or three in the first month and then once a month thereafter), "reasonable" telephone/email contact with the coach, a post-coaching report. So, the usual is around eight sessions over six months, but they can be as few as four or as many as 20, depending on the range and depth of the agenda. Another way of charging is to make the fee 10 percent or 15 percent of the annual salary of the client. That can be serious cash, of course.

How long does each session last?

Sessions usually last for 90 minutes, though they can easily run to two hours, depending on the stamina of both parties. For most coaches, the time passes remarkably quickly – after all, it is all about them.

What factors most influence how a coach charges?

There are two types of answers: semi-factual (seniority of clients, how much control executives have over the budget, solo/one-man-band vs employee of coaching firm); and the rather cynical narcissism and greed of the coach. Many charge simply according to how much they think the organization can bear; others the biggest number they can say without smiling.

Market forces can come into play ... but not often, as it is such a secretive business.

Does the size of the fee affect the process or outcome?

In guarded moments, most coaches say "no," but they may add: "If you had a significant illness, would you choose the cheapest doctor?" Most of us have seen those consumer reports on various products – everything from pesto to port – and have been surprised by the complete lack of relationship between brand, price and evaluation.

So what does determine the outcome? The skill of the coach? The educability of the coachee? The timing of the coaching? The type of coaching offered? Perhaps. But it could be the well-known placebo, or even Hawthorne, effect.

All counseling, coaching and therapy works for some very simple reasons. *First*, As a result of their coaching, clients receive acceptance, attention, care, respect and support. It is this sense of being understood and assisted that is essential to a feeling of well-being and effectiveness. *Second*, the whole process encourages greater self-monitoring and self-analysis, which often, in-and-of itself, suggests solutions. *Third*, clients often report being happier and more optimistic because they believe their coping mechanisms and strategies have improved. And the employment of a coach is often reaffirmation of commitment to change, which is the best predictor of change.

Maybe the size of the invoice makes one stick at it all the more.

51 The requirements of good managers

Every organization understands that it needs to recruit and retain talented leaders for the future.

A central question in this quest is to know what one is looking for and, secondly, how to assess or measure it. Five factors come up again and again.

Cognitive ability: the single best predictor of leadership/management success is intelligence, particularly at higher levels of management. This is not to be confused with formal education, though they are modestly related. Managers need to be *bright enough*: that is, they require some minimum level of intelligence to do the job well. As one goes up within the organization, jobs become more complex. Further, things can change or need changing, and leaders have to understand those issues. Followers like, respect and support brighter leaders. Brighter leaders are both seen as, and are, more effective than less bright leaders. Brighter leaders are better at transforming organizations and managing change. Brighter leaders have more (intellectual) self-confidence and suffer less stress. Brighter leaders learn faster, are more positive about personal growth and are more adaptable.

Emotional adjustment and stability: senior management and leadership positions always involve stress. People have to make hard decisions, take risks, face criticism and setbacks. They need to be hardy and resilient to take the pace and challenges of modern business life. Less stable people are, in essence, prone to neuroses. Unstable people tend to be tense, touchy and thin-skinned. They can have rapidly fluctuating moods and be very brittle.

In short: unstable people are prone to anxiety and depression. They are particularly vulnerable to stress and stress-related illness. Neurosis is related to absenteeism. Unstable people can be self-pitying, self-defeating and prone to a depressive, gloomy outlook. Followers report having considerable difficulty with the moodiness and vulnerability of unstable managers. Stable leaders, by contrast, cope well under inevitable periods of stress. Stable leaders tend to have healthy adaptable coping strategies, whereas the opposite is true for their less-able colleagues.

The work ethic and conscientiousness: every business leader needs to be hard-working; self-disciplined leaders have to be dependable, reliable and responsible. They need to be responsive to various stakeholders – their staff, colleagues, customers and shareholders. They have to learn to be efficient and organized. They need to understand the need to plan ahead and to ensure things are always done to the required standard.

Conscientiousness is closely related to competence, which is one of the highest-rated virtues followers want in their managers. Conscientiousness is also related to dedication, deliberation and dutifulness. Conscientious leaders are hard-working, but they learn to work "smart" as well as to work long hours. They understand when and why they need to go the extra mile. Conscientious leaders tend to be achievement-oriented and aspirational for themselves and others. Conscientious leaders deliver on their promises, which are realistic, and they tend to follow ethical rules sensibly and sensitively.

Emotional intelligence, social skills and charm: management and leadership is a social activity. Leaders have to inspire and support their staff. They are in the motivation business. Emotional intelligence, in essence, involves understanding and being able to influence other people. But it also involves self-understanding or awareness, and the knowledge of how to deal with setbacks. Emotional intelligence is, essentially, about having social skills, charm and insight. Emotionally intelligent leaders understand the importance and power of emotions in everyday life. They are good at the emotional regulation of everyday life. We know emotionally intelligent leaders are liked, trusted and admired most by their staff.

Leaders with a high EQ always get the best out of their staff and are, hence, highly productive. High-EQ leaders are particularly successful in difficult times when organizations are under considerable pressure. They understand the important psychological needs of their key staff members, and are very good at getting the best out of them. Emotional intelligence is linked to being more assertive, empathic, optimistic and self-motivated.

Motivation, drive, the need to achieve: motivation is the engine of leadership success, but it needs direction. People are quite clearly motivated by different things – power, influence, control, recognition. The great problem with the concept of motivation is that it appears, at the same time, all encompassing and vague. People are motivated to achieve a goal: the more motivated they are, the more time, effort and energy they are willing to put into achieving that goal. More importantly, most of these goals are not easily satisfied; and this motivation does not stop once they have been achieved. This is true of both psychological goals (like recognition) and more objective goals (like monetary reward).

We know that all people are motivated to seek recognition and reward from those they work for in order to boost their self-esteem. Motivated leaders are often particularly sensitive to issues around fairness – that is, that reward is directly related to effort, that output and input are closely linked.

Motivated leaders have realistic expectations, and set for themselves and others attainable but stretched goals. Motivated leaders are less distracted by setbacks. Motivated leaders learn from their mistakes and direct their efforts most efficiently.

52 Restorative justice at work

Every so often, we read about new ways to rehabilitate prisoners by making them face their victims. There are also various calls for victims to be more involved in setting punishments, rather than leaving it up to the law enforcers. Few crimes are victimless. Whilst at work, most people would argue it's much more acceptable (and common) to steal from one's employer than a colleague – liberating stationery is quite different from dipping into the till or another person's wallet. And then there is stealing from the customer by over-charging or under-delivering.

Most people in business are quite rightly concerned with minimizing these problems. Some see it as a selection and security issue, believing the cause to be bad people abusing lax systems. Their preference is for lie detectors or integrity tests at selection and a great deal of surveillance at work. Others see these negative behaviors as more to do with managers alienating and generally upsetting staff, who take revenge in the easiest way. There, prevention is through improving the way managers are trained.

There is another issue, however: how wrong-doers are dealt with in organizations. This is a big issue in schools and in tight communities. Is bullying at school really much different from bullying at work? Don't playground bullies go on to become office bullies? Does the exam cheat not also cheat on his boss, colleagues and partner? That's debatable: but the question is, how to deal with wrong-doers?

It has become fashionable to contrast two very different approaches to crime, delinquency and deviance, be they at school or work. It is the contrast between *retributive* and *restorative* justice. The former sees "misbehavior" in terms of breaking the law, the rules or the conventions; the latter as adversely affecting many other people.

The retributive approach focuses on establishing blame or guilt, often through some adversarial process. It is believed that the evidence argued over by prosecution and defense will (hopefully, usually) establish who did what and when, and perhaps why. There may be, as part of this model, a great deal of attention to due processes: following carefully and openly the proper procedures that ensure justice. It's a model that emphasizes head over heart: where argument and conflict of description and explanation are portrayed as abstract, impersonal and logical.

The restorative justice model involves many more people: pretty well all or any who were affected by the behavior: the "victim," their friends and family, witnesses even. Their task is twofold: to express their feelings but, more importantly, a problem-solving attempt to prevent recurrence.

The retributive model aims to deter by some sort of punishment: pain, exclusion, firing. The restitution model aims for the restoration of property and well-being by reconciliation. It is usually much more about relationships, respect and feelings. It's not about the pain that the perpetrator should receive but, rather, the pain the victims feel. It's less about meting out the exact and appropriate amount of pain for that inflicted, and more about repairing the damage, hurt or injury to others.

In the retributive model, the community (school, workplace) within which the problem has occurred sees justice done by being on the jury or being spectators to the whole process. Hence, the importance of the representativeness of juries. The restorative model is rather more vague. Any and all of those in the community can, and should, be involved in the restorative project because all are involved.

Finally, there is the role of the wrong-doer. In the retributive model, it is they who accept the punishment as "fair exchange" for their crime and as a deterrent to others. In the restorative model, it's all about fully understanding the impact of their actions – all of the consequences of the act – and deciding how best to put things right.

So, the more traditional model is about apportioning blame, the analysis of motives and decisions about punishment. The restorative approach is more about establishing who has been affected and how, how to put things right and what can be learnt from the process.

So, pie-in-the-sky, silver bullet, psychobabble nonsense? Never heard of psychopaths, criminal gangs or sadistic bullies? Interesting, but can't see how it applies to work?

How any organization deals with misdemeanors sends very powerful messages. Some prefer a cover-up, others a very public display of retribution. Some misdemeanors seem more abstractly victimless than others, such as theft or fraud – but how about interpersonal violence? Some people are traumatized for long periods. Would this help their recovery? Would you prefer to be tried by a judge and two assessors or a jury of your peers? Or a jury of your victims?

Ask wrong-doers if they would prefer to do a week or a month of community service or meet their victims and their families face-to-face. Offer them a chance to repair and restore goodwill or be sacked, go to prison or whatever. An easy option? Perhaps. Was it chance that the Pope visited his potential assassin. Here, the victim offers the perpetrator help to restore the crime.

Could all this work at work? Worth having a go.

53 Sack 'em all

Which three departments or sections of your organization do you loathe the most? Do others share your view? Would you happily see the whole section sacked, removed entirely or out-sourced? And, more importantly, if given the push, is it possible that nobody would notice?

There are many criteria for disliking, despising or demeaning different functions in the organization. Some are considered to be doing merely trivial work – like the personnel relations department. Others are considered a general nuisance, such as security. Still others represent a serious handicap to getting on with the job – for example, HR.

It is usually possible to distinguish between two broad sections of any organization: production vs. process; fee earners vs. support; front-of-house vs. backroom. Whilst, for some functions, the area is rather grey (e.g. finance), most people understand the difference. But the difference perception of the two areas is rather dramatic. Fee earners view at least some of their support staff as unnecessary, pointless and, worse still, a drain on the organization. They see them as "taxing" the organization, and have funny names for them: the "sales prevention department" or "Human Remains."

By contrast, the support staff may characterize those whom they serve or service as unappreciative, egocentric and naïve. So, some organizations do their best to try to prevent animosity occurring between those two groups. They do this in a variety of ways: they may give them different titles (like "central support"), which rather clouds the issue at least from an outsider's perspective. They may attempt some structural method such as matrix management, or they may try physical or architectural ways of ensuring that groups are not physically – and therefore psychologically – separated.

Despite all of these efforts, there remains a great deal of internal animosity in most organizations. However, there is a general consensus about which section is most disliked. The three departments that are nearly always most nominated are, *first*, HR; *second*, security; *third*, finance. This rank order may differ as a function of the history and size of the company and other factors, which include the location of the health and safety department.

The question arises as to why these functions are so universally disliked. Is it the sort of people who are attracted to them in the first place? Is it the way they carry out their tasks? Is it that they have to be the disciplinarians, regulators and proscribers of acceptable and unacceptable behavior to the wild boys and girls in the organization? Organizations vary with regard to the size and power of different departments. There are some "recommended" business ratios, such as 80:1 for HR – that is, for every 80 staff (perhaps beyond a certain level) you have one HR professional. But organizational history has meant that some have very large, very small, or even non-existent departments of various sizes.

Nearly always top of the list for being happily voted out of the office by staff is HR. Why? Several theories have been put forward, one eloquently written and well-quoted piece called "Why I hate HR." Some HR functions are pretty crucial, including payroll and compliance. But the contact most people have with HR is through paperwork. There is nothing like being forced to comply with some seemingly meaningless, time-consuming, alienating and – worse – guru-fashionable task to upset people. Say the words "performance appraisal," "climate survey" or "diversity training" and listen to the reactions. Does it have to be like this?

Could it be argued that the principles of performance management and all that goes with it are simply those of good management? Because poor managers can't or won't engage with performance management; they have to be coerced into doing so. It's the coercion, manipulation and mandating they hate most.

Perhaps therein lies the issue: coercion. Are the professionals we dislike the most those who apparently curb our freedom or regiment us in ways we hate? Hence the loathing, in particular, of health and safety – perceived as the fetishistic killjoys of business. Equally loathed are the security staff – seen as the suited bouncers or petty tyrants of the building.

HR make you fill out forms, security make you wear passes, the finance department demands accountability. So, why not "sack em all"?

Animosity against "service" departments can cause problems. HR people constantly agonize about their role and importance. It has been the theme of a hundred conferences and books. They fret about the fact that many HR directors often don't sit on the board. Not that relevant, you see.

The top security people rarely worry as much. They know why they are there. Life's a little easier to explain. They give as good as they get.

And finance know that they really are essential. They pull it all together. They supposedly know the real costs of everything and can explain it all.

How many people from HR or security make it to CEO? They sure do in finance. Why? Is it because of their training, background or interests? Those departments or specialities that seem despised or disliked need to be able to articulate a good "business case" for their existence. This involves more than a quote or statistic from some dodgy outdated business book. They need to prove their worth or face the sack.

54   Segmenting the sat nav market

Sat nav is a must have: A sexy, "flash in the pan" toy, or a serious bit of business kit one can't do without? Clearly, the latter – and, dare one say it, perhaps particularly useful for the fairer sex, who have demonstrably shown themselves to be less good on a range of spatial tasks like map reading!? Or maybe the traveling rep who can't drive and map-read simultaneously?

It's odd to believe that orbiting spacecraft designed for the Cold War are helping you around the back-streets of Tooting Beck, and that satellites in space know precisely how to get around Tulsa, Oklahoma.

There are different models of sat nav, and there are already different options. You can change the voice: male vs. female; sexy vs. authoritarian; native vs. foreign.

But the sat nav designers have, so far, missed a trick. They have not yet designed specialized or customized sat nav systems for specialist drivers. We know people drive as they live. And we know that people lead very different lives.

So, what about sat nav? Intuitively, it appears that five or six different models need designing.

The nervous driver: insecure, anxious, prone to depression and moody, the nervous driver needs reassurance. Sat nav could be a counseling device. So, once the postcode has been keyed in, it might say: "Go on – you can do it." Or you could have the non-directive one: "How do you feel about the journey?" After each correct execution of the left or right turn, how about "Well done; you're doing well." The worst times are when the voice goes silent in the long bits where you are required just to follow the road. These may easily be interpreted as disapproving, cold judgmental silences where nanny is not really approving of your driving skill. So, here we need the counselor's reassuring voice that all is well. Thus, every minute at least, we need "We are doing well," "Excellent progress" and "Not far now, nearly there."

The boy racer: this needs a masculine, blokeish voice and attitude. "At the next junction turn left" becomes "Hang a left." The boy racer wants to know how and when and where to go faster. The trip is a game, a challenge to manhood – a hunt. So, the voice needs to be programmed to flatter the road-holding, cornering, smooth acceleration and smart overtaking of cautious Lada drivers. The sat nav must be a mate not a crutch. It must do blokey, non-PC talk. "Get a move on China" or "Get your arse into gear for the next roundabout." Jolly good fun to write the script. A sure-fire seller.

The obsessional: the quality-control, health-and-safety-type driver wants exact detail and more feedback than machines currently supply. And none of this "in 800 yards" vagueness – "in 820 yards" is much better. Obsessionals need to get it right: first time and exactly. So, once they have programmed the machine, they need to know it is right. The voice may repeat the destination. Some obsessionals need to know their general direction, so how about "in 745 yards turn left (an 11 o'clock turn), so that we are now proceeding east-south-east on the A204 to Great Winterbottom. The road, first constructed in 1947, has recently been resurfaced and has excellent grip." The voice should be clear and exacting. Remember: obsessionals have concerns with time, cleanliness, orderliness and parsimony. Build it in.

The believer: religious motorists, too, have their special needs. How about a satnav that does a quick motorist's prayer immediately as one sets off? And the voice? Modulated Anglican with plain chant cadence; or hellfire Southern Baptist/Ulster Methodist, or even Arabic Imam. Believers will imbue the device with supernatural powers. After all, the signals are coming from the heavens. They will obey. How about on the straight bits a "We will, God willing, be there shortly and safely." How about short bursts of music during the downtimes. Perhaps *For those in peril on the sea* or *Onward Christian soldiers*. But most important is the end of the journey announcement. None of this "Your journey terminates here" or "You have reached your final destination." Much better "We give thanks for our sound and safe arrival this day, and hope, that in all future travels and travails, we will overcome all obstacles and barriers to arrive at our chosen destination."

The rap artist: there must be a warning on the box because rap is, for some, a foreign tongue. It may be the hardest model to build. But what an opportunity for a struggling artist from the inner city! This is sat nav with attitude and with beat. The music continues during the long, on-track bits with hypnotic rhythm.

The gadgeteer: This is the state-of-the-art, early-adopter's model. The graphics are hyper-realistic, the sound effects stunning and the options unlimited. It does weather and traffic and directions all at once. So, this is sat nav with features and extras. This is sat nav that could be programmed to meet the particular peccadilloes of the particular gadgeteer who can show off his (yes, definitely his) odd quirks to others.

All marketing people know about segmentation. They know how important it is to understand psycho-ideographical groups to both pitch and adapt the product. Managers could think likewise with other equipment in the office.

55 Selecting a prime minister or president

What characteristics do we want in our next prime minister or President? Below is a good shortlist of competencies to put the fear into any challengers. Three select-ins and three select-outs. Insufficient evidence of the former and too much of the latter means NO.

Select for:

Integrity: this is honesty, trustworthiness, truthfulness. At some level, you must be able to trust that what is being said is true. It takes courage to maintain integrity in politics and business. It is the single characteristic that people most want in a boss.

Intelligence: this is more than street-smarts. It is being analytic, logical, quick-on-the-uptake. We have plenty of evidence of the shortcomings of the short-changed. Where people were educated is not a good indication of intelligence any more. There's nothing like an under-powered leader, even with a bright team around them, to slow things down.

Inspirational: the ability to be uplifting, enthusiastic, positive ... to create and sustain a following. All the more important in our multi-media age. This more than reading auto-cues. At best, this is charisma; at worst, it's the ability to give good speeches.

Select out

Irresponsibility: evidence of amoral, impulsive, selfish behavior in the past that was more to do with fulfilling personal ambition than anything else. A good measure is how many friends the person has retained from past worlds (school, work, family). It's about a social conscience: looking after more than just "number 1."

Excessive self-confidence: clear evidence of a narcissistic streak manifested in everything from dress to the number and types of individuals chosen to serve their personal needs. Good self-aware, high self-esteem is good: narcissism very dangerous.

Susceptability to stress: it's tough at the top. A leader needs to be hardy not moody; resilient not unstable. The anxious, depressed or psychosomatically ill leader makes bad decisions. They are unpredictable and moody. Hard to work for and live with. A definite no-no.

This list could fit many different senior positions. So, are there unique competencies and characteristics for the job of the leader of the country? This person clearly needs to be able and stable, hard-working and hardy. But then, there is the sticky issue of values. After all, politics is supposed to be informed by values, what we used to call "ideology" – nowadays, the "vision thing."

Focus groups and opinion polls seem to shape government policy more than values these days. Hence the difficulty in finding the "clear blue water" between the parties that seem to converge more and more in the minds of many.

But, looking back at the most famous British prime ministers – like Churchill, Wilson and Thatcher, it is evident they marched to a very clear ideological drum. There are many ways to try to categorize values that relate to the "socialism vs. conservatism," "equality vs. freedom" rhetoric found in party political manifestos of old.

Selectors talk of values such as **recognition** (the desire to be noticed, visible, seen to be in charge), **power** (the desire to make things happen, make a difference), **altruism** (the desire to help others, serve the community), **security** (a desire to make things predictable, safe, secure) and **tradition** (a belief in old-fashioned institutions and virtues). There are social, economic and political values.

But it's very easy to "fake" value-talk. All politicians are skilled at and trained in the dark art of performing on cultural affairs and politics programs.

Candidates are sought for the office of prime minister/president.

Applicants should be bright and inspirational, with a high degree of integrity. Irresponsible, excessively self-confident and stress-prone individuals need not apply. The successful candidate will ideally be a conviction politician.

Salary: high average, perks considerable.

56　Servant leadership

There have been at least four historical themes in the way people have thought and written about leadership. The first, which still pervades, is the "**great man**" trait theories, which argue that leaders have particular qualities or attributes that enable them to do the job. The next phase concentrated on the leader's **style** of leading. It was called the "**behavioral approach**" and looked at how, for instance, democratic and authoritarian and *laissez-faire* leaders went about the job. You choose your style.

The third approach, popular from the 1950s to the 1970s, stressed the situational determinant of leadership: "**cometh the hour, cometh the man.**" There are different leaders for different situations: war vs. peace, growth vs. decline, change vs stability. Then we had the fourth phase: the emergence of the charismatic, future-oriented, **transformational** leader, contrasted with the steady-as-you-go **transactional** manager.

But that is all old hat. That was the 1980s. What's new in this low-cost-to-entry school of leadership studies? Quite a lot, really. Well, quite a lot of buzz words. We have had "organic" leadership, and "empowered" leadership, and "primitive" leadership. We have "tele"-leadership. And "authentic" leadership. We have had a close examination of a host of remarkable historical figures, like Shackleton, to understand their methods and philosophy.

One of the new-ish ideas is the curious, almost oxymoron, **servant leadership**. The ideas are not that new but have been repackaged and chime nicely with the current zeitgeist. This hardly new idea is that the leader serves the people that he or she leads. What they are supposed to do is focus on the individual complex and changing needs of all these that they lead. Their primary task is coaching and development. They are there to facilitate individual personal growth and to build a strong sense of community. And, hopefully, keep an eye on the bottom line.

Servant leaders are particularly effective – it is argued – because the needs of followers mean they reach their full potential and, hence, perform at their best.

The servant leaders, said Robert Greenleaf, the author of the book *The Servant as Leader*, has the primary task of making those underneath him healthier, wiser, freer and more autonomous. He or she must be the primary example of the caring, ethical teacher.

Servant leaders are, it is decreed, committed to develop various characteristics/skills in themselves and others – like awareness, conceptualization and building community. You can even do a test (devised by John Barbuto and Daniel Wheeler (2006), who specialized in the topic) to work out if you are one already. Score seven "yes"es to the following adapted quiz, and you are a certified servant leader:

- Do most people believe that you are willing to sacrifice your own self-interest for the good of the group you lead?
- Do people believe that you really want to hear their ideas, as well as value them and act upon them?
- Do people believe that you will understand what is really happening in their lives – the joys and pains they experience as a function of working for you?
- Do people come to you, for advice, counseling and support when the chips are down or when something traumatic has happened in their lives?
- Do others believe that you have a strong intuitive awareness for what is going on at work, especially the people issues?
- Do others follow your commands, instructions and requests because they want to, as opposed to because they fear the consequences of not doing so?
- Do others communicate their ideas, hopes and vision for their part and the whole organization when you are around?
- Do others seem to have confidence in your ability to anticipate and plan for the future, and ensure health and longevity of the organization?
- Do others believe you are running the organization so as to make a positive difference for all stakeholders?
- Do people believe that you are committed to helping them personally develop, grow and fulfill their potential?
- Do people feel a strong sense of community, loyalty and dedication in the organization that you lead?

A nicely corrective pendulum serving against autocratic, hierarchical leadership, or impractical, sentimental tosh likely to bankrupt an organization.

The central question must be is the nature and the purpose of any company. If servant leaders believed they were servants to the shareholders, the whole emphasis might be quite different. Private organizations are in business: they succeed or fail by making money. Their end is profit. The aim is to give shareholders a reasonable return on their investment. No investment – no company. No company – no workers. No workers – no nothing.

The servant-leader model is based on numerous wrong axioms, let alone what the central purpose of business leadership is all about. The most important is the invalid assumption that the satisfied worker is more productive, as opposed to the productive worker being more satisfied.

No problem with coaching, developing, growing, teaching, training staff. But the purpose of this growing activity is ultimately to make them more productive.

The job of a leader is not to be a personal coach or a psychotherapist. Their job is to select and manage: to set clear stretching goals, to help their staff achieve those goals by giving feedback and support; to build dynamic, focused, effective teams to deliver them.

The opposite of leaders as masters is not leaders as servants. Neither work in the long term. If leaders thought of themselves servants to their shareholders, the whole thing might be a good deal more sensible.

57 Seven steps to happiness

What do business gurus, psychiatrists, theologians and economists have in common? One thing is that they are all expected to provide the answer to the question: "What makes people really happy?" How to achieve maximal well-being, fulfillment, authenticity and even joyfulness in life?

The curiously reassuring thing is that the answers are so similar. Certainly, many have changed their minds over time, particularly naïve materialistic economists given to simple formulae.

Some still hold onto the notion of happy genes and the "happy personality profile." The idea is that there are predispositional factors that contribute to happiness. That may well be true, but genes interact with the environment and express themselves in different ways. Those born bright, attractive and healthy to a middle-class family in a stable democracy have a better chance. Or do they? Check out the suicide or depression statistics. Just as we make our luck, we also make our happiness.

So, what are the seven steps? Broadly, they can fall into three groups: those about time, about people and about thoughts.

The *first* step is simple: "*carpe diem*." Live in the now. Celebrate, use, enjoy today as if it were the last day in your life. Seize opportunities, default on "yes;" revel in the moment; life is not a dress rehearsal.

The *second* step is also time related. **Let go the past**. Easier said than done. The monkey on the shoulder. What is most interesting about this issue is that one implication is **not** to go into a therapy or counseling that tries to help adjustment and encourage happiness by raking over the coals of the past. Imprisonment not liberation, many report. The idea is not to be chained by emotions or beliefs that happened a long time ago. "The past is a foreign country: they do things differently there." Happiness, insight, forgiveness and reconciliation are not the same. Look forward, not back.

Third, there are the people issues. The third step is to **join groups** involved in projects. Sartre was wrong: happiness, not hell, is other people. Sure, it does depend on who they are. Happy people are heart-lifting, life-enhancing as much as unhappy people are heart-sinking. We are social animals. We are designed to live in groups; to chatter and natter; give social support: care about each other. Your social networking only becomes functionally noteworthy when you lose it. Unemployed and retired people often become depressed because they are deprived of their friends at work.

Fourth, do **voluntary** work. There is much available, and this can be anything from helping serve in a local charity shop to collecting money, helping strangers or whatever. People say you can't motivate people if you don't pay them. But volunteer workers are often amongst the most happy. The work gives them purpose. It provides time, structure and a sense of self-worth.

Fifth, **pursue a passion** by learning or upgrading a skill. Most of us have gifts, though it does often take quite some time to discover what they are. It is never too late to polish up some talent. The passion does not, however, need to be skill related. It may be collecting or even train-spotting. But it gives *flow*: that state where total absorption means time is forgotten. It is the most perfect of states.

Sixth, the steps involving thoughts or cognitive skills. They refer to the way we think about issues. The sixth step to happiness is to **count your blessings**. The old saying went: "I cried because I had no shoes, and then I saw a man who had no feet." It can be very unhealthy and unhappy-making, indulging in what is called upward comparison; that is, comparing ourselves with those much better off. More attractive, richer, more powerful. But downward comparisons can be seriously beneficial. Most of us have a great deal to be grateful for. We need reminding of that.

Finally, **act and think** positive. Call it "cognitive behavioral therapy" or the "art of making friends and influencing people." It's about starting positive, virtuous cycles – not negative, vicious circles. There are two sorts of consequences. If you smile, others are likely to also – making all interaction easier. Further, there is some evidence of biochemical feedback loops. It's all that stuff about endorphins. Acting positively leads to lowered stress, which leads to feeling more relaxed and positive, which leads to greater happiness for all concerned.

So, start the journey. Take the steps. Today is the first day of the rest of your life. You can be and stay happy. But you have to practice.

58 Sex at work

Perhaps the oddest thing about sex is that we can now all talk about it a great deal, but still "do it" under very restricted circumstances. Serious newspapers have therapists telling it to us straight. Sex education is mandatory in schools. But sex at work – talk or action – is a serious no-no. We can talk about, and are encouraged to accept, numerous variants of sexual preferences, but sexual jokes or conversations remain something you can't discuss or practice in the office. And the act of "fun and frolics" in the office is really very, very unacceptable … even at the Christmas party in the stationary cupboard.

Taboo, prohibition and secrecy are the agents of ignorance. How can we be an empathic, compassionate and informed society without open discussions? Are there sex-related psychiatric disorders that go unnoticed and untreated? Perhaps, paradoxically, we have become a repressed society; slaves to political correctness.

Maybe all the sexual drives have had to be sublimated into a strange array of quasi acceptable behaviors. Could we need a neo-Freudian understanding of the modern office? 'Twas he who said we spend a great deal of energy dealing with those two most powerful and primitive of drives: sex and aggression.

The following is a "first draft" of possible problems stalking the modern office: it shows how sex pervades all aspects of our life:

Anticipatory appraisal aversion: this is a deep – almost visceral – loathing and phobia associated with having to conduct appraisals on diffident, difficult or doomed staff. Total aversion is the major cause of performance management virginity. Common in techies, IT and engineering.

Board member frottage: this is similar to **ostentatious osmotic dependency**. It is the delusional belief that (literally) "rubbing up against" powerful board members gives one special powers, privileges and promotional opportunities. Sort of business groupies.

Bonus fantasy paraphilia: the sad person with this experiences intensely arousing visions of obscenely large bonus payments occurring after a strictly average year. This can cause unmitigated distress and is incurable.

Chronic premature articulation: this is the constant urge to speak before

1. Knowing what one wants to say.
2. Being asked to speak.
3. Considering the consequences of career-limiting, egocentric, business babble.

Common in marketing and sales: poor prognosis.

Competitor strategy voyeurism: the uncontrollable obsession with what others are doing in the marketplace. It can lead to **eye-off-the-ball myopia**. It is about web-surfing very obscure and rather naughty sites in the hope of gleaning supposedly competitor knowledge. Addictive.

Dysfunctional conference exhibitionism: this is linked to **adolescent show-off impulses**, involving self-obsessed narcissistic displays of emotion and heroic personal stories at all conferences. Crying is acceptable … perhaps compulsory. Requires anecdotes about family members.

Health and safety sado-masochism: this is the unrelenting and unforgiving urge to inflict pain on oneself and others, possibly alternating, by being difficult-to-impossible about locked doors, temperature gauges and access. It is linked to **security-compulsive disorder**.

Hyper- or hypo-active six-ual desire: the former is the more common complaint and revolves around the obscenely early (in terms of years) desire and demand to be paid a six-figure salary. Hypo-active desire occurs after years of failure and a preference to waste energy sniping at others who succeed.

New sexy logo obsession: a corporate police issue where every document, PowerPoint presentation and internal memo must contains the new (very expensive) logo in the right colors, at the right angle and in the right place to "sex-up" the business and double profits.

Office supplier fetishism: this may be manifest in curious ways – spending hours poring over stationery catalogues; sniffing certain products;

prohibiting the use of some items and prescribing the compulsory use of others on irrational grounds.

Open-plan screen erectile dysfunction: this is the inability to erect sufficiently tall screens in an open-plan office to create the altogether natural and satisfying feeling that one is in closed-plan surroundings again. This may be caused by strict nannies with rules about big erections in the office.

Premature promotion syndrome: this is characterized as a youthful disorder where young people are not prepared to "do their time" among the troops, wanting senior manager status long before their time.

Vice-president identity disorder: this is caused by working for one of those mid-Atlantic organizations where everybody is an executive vice-president. It results in not really knowing if one is important or not, but very clearly nothing to do with vice except in the metalwork sense.

Virtual team vaginisimus: this is a fear and phobia of the V-word – knowing that virtual is virtually nothing. It can result from trying bizarre email or phone brainstorming groups with bleary-eyed New Zealanders or bewildered Japanese at odd times of the day.

Wash-room gossip arousal: this is akin to **luvvy-lavvy excitement** and results from the realization that the best grapevine is found in the office toilets, where literally pissed-off managers pour out their venom about the grown-ups.

Work-life, boardroom–bedroom balance aversion: this is caused by the shocking realization that one is better off staying at work with all the power and structure processes in place than going home where chaos rules. It is a strictly "males only" problem.

59 Shapers of destiny

All successful leaders provide much the same narrative of the factors that influenced them the most. Studies across organizations in different sectors, as well as those within big corporations, and across different corporate and national cultures, even different historical time zones, reveal the same story. This is now so clear that academics, somewhat uncharacteristically, call for no further work to be done on this area.

Again and again, leaders mention six powerful learning experiences that shaped their vision, taught them powerful lessons and caught their imagination. Be they famous for start-ups or turnarounds, be they great captains of industry or mega rich entrepreneurs, or be they well-known or respected leaders in government, education or the military, the factors are the same.

The *first* is **early work experience**. This may be a "part-time" Saturday job at school; a relatively unskilled summer holiday job at university; or one of the first jobs they ever had. For some, it was the unadulterated tedium or monotony that powerfully motivated them never to have to do those jobs, and taught them to appreciate others who do them. For others, it was a particular work style or process that they have retained all their lives.

Many people have "false starts," "try-outs" or "first goes" to see where their passions and interests match their ability and talents. For many, work comes as a bit of a shock: following the strict time schedules, witnessing widespread pilfering, union–management distrust and dislike. Its memory sticks at an impressionable age.

The *second* factor is the **experience of other people** and is nearly always an immediate boss, but can be a colleague or one of the serious grown-ups. They are almost always remembered as either very bad or very good: both teach lessons. What always – or never – to do. Just as we parent as we were parented, so many manage as they were managed. Unless, of course, there is a model to suggest otherwise.

Some people vow never to repeat the negative, humiliating control-freakery of an early boss. Others remember and try to copy the guide, mentor and supervisor who taught them so much. It's a bit like the inspirational teacher who changed pupils for life: who gave one confidence, excited the imagination and made work fun. Or, of course, the one who within a few weeks succeeded in putting pupils off cricket or chemistry forever.

The *third* factor is **short-term assignments**: project work, standing in for another, or interim management. Because this takes people out of their comfort zone and exposes them to issues and problems they have never before confronted, they learn quickly. For some, it is the lucky break: serendipity provides an opportunity to find a new skill or passion.

Fourth – but, for many, top of the list – is the **first major line assignment**. This is often the first promotion, foreign posting or departmental move to a higher position. It is often frequently cited because suddenly the stakes were higher, everything more complex and novel and ambiguous. There was more pressure: the buck stopped here. You were accountable. Suddenly, the difficulties of management became real.

The *fifth* factor can be subsumed under the above for many. It is **hardships of various kinds**. It is about attempting to cope in a crisis that may be professional or personal. It teaches the real value of things: technology, loyal staff, supportive head offices. The experiences are those of battle-hardened soldiers, or the "been there, done that" brigade.

Hardship teaches many lessons: how resourceful and robust some people can be, and how others panic and cave in. It teaches some to admire a fit and happy organization when they see it. It teaches them to distinguish needs and wants. It teaches a little about minor forms of post-traumatic stress disorder. And the virtues of stoicism, hardiness and a tough mental attitude.

Lower down on the list comes the **management development** stuff. Some remember and quote their MBA experience; far fewer, some specific (albeit fiendishly expensive) course. One or two quote the experience of receiving 360-degree feedback. More recall a coach, either because they were so good or so awful.

Rather bad news for trainers, business school teachers and coaches. Here is the bottom line from this research and the implications of it. To the extent that leadership is acquired, developed and learnt, rather than "gifted," it is achieved mainly through work experiences. Inevitably, some experiences are better than others because they teach different lessons in different ways. And some people seem to acquire these valuable experiences despite, rather than as a result of, company policy.

Experiential learning takes time, but timing is important. It's not a steady, planned accumulation of insights and skills. Some experiences teach little or, indeed, bad habits.

But three factors conspire to defeat the experiential model. *First*, both young managers and their bosses want to short-circuit experience: learn faster, cheaper, better. Hence the appeal of the one-minute manager, the one-day MBA and the short course. *Second*, many HR professionals see this approach as disempowering them, because they are "in charge" of the leadership development program. *Third*, some see experience as a test, not a developmental exercise.

So, maybe leadership potential and talent should be defined as the "ability to learn from experience." Additionally, every move, promotion or challenge should also be assessed from the perspective of its learning potential.

60   So, what is potential?

Sadly, "talent management" in many organizations is based on people not always with much salient knowledge making highly dubious ratings on others' performance and potential. Talent management, it is said, is all about four things: how to **attract**, **develop**, **deploy** and **retain** talented people. Indeed, but hardest of all is to identify the talent in the first place. How do you know talent when you see it? And what happened to all those talented classmates at school and university: where are they now?

For some time, the talent industry has recommended that you define talent by two criteria. Two ratings of how those people are currently performing at work (from low to high) and how much potential they seem to have. The wunderkinder, the golden group, the talented are "high–high:" rated very positively on both dimensions. The "low–low" should be managed out, the "low potential–OK performance" fixed at their level; and the "high potential–low performance" seriously investigated.

Whilst it may seem that the rating of performance levels is reliable and straightforward, it soon becomes apparent how problematic it is. It's easy to measure sales (revenue, sales calls, profits), but to measure a young executive, a junior officer, a junior doctor? Much of the disillusion with appraisals, and performance management in particular, lies in the difficulty of the measurement (note: not rating) of potential.

We all know the consequence of announcing simple behavioral measures. Bus drivers who refuse to pick up passengers or who care little about fare dodgers because they are only measured on time-keeping. The police who discourage the reporting of certain crimes because they know they are unlikely to solve them and the "clear-up role" is the performance criterion. Hospital staff who take wheels off trolleys because they then become beds can happily fulfill government criteria about patients being admitted into hospital at certain periods. Often, the more complex, cerebral and administrative the job, the harder it is to measure. Of course, ratings are very different. Some people are quite happy to rate others on the very limited knowledge they have.

Some organizations try and improve the reliability of ratings by getting numerous senior people to rate someone they know (or think they know).

What often surprises is the difference between ratings. This is sometimes caused by rating styles. Rater *Softly* is too generous on every criterion to everyone. Rater *Midway* thinks everybody is average – no one is good, no one weak. Rater *Nasty* is a mean bastard who thinks everyone (no doubt, bar himself) is a mediocre idler.

Ratings, like contact lenses, are in the eye of the beholder, rather than in the behavior of the rated. It takes time to teach people how to do ratings accurately, reliably and with sufficient differentiation between the good and the bad. They need to know what behaviors they are looking for and what they mean, and actually collect the data. They need specific ratings that differentiate within and between individuals.

But forget performance ratings, let's try potential. What on earth does potential really mean? Potential is an actuarial trajectory. Most people assume implicitly that it is the ability to be effective at a higher level in organizational roles. It is the possibility that a person can become something much more than they currently are. Talent is a competitive advantage. Yeah, yeah, yeah – but that does not help with the ratings.

How about: *potential* is an interest in learning and applying knowledge and skills in an organizational context, together with the ability to do so. Now, perhaps, we are getting somewhere. Potential requires that talented people want to explore and exploit their talent. This is more than simple ambition and drive to be rich, powerful and successful. It can mean hard graft and dedication. Every talented sports person or musician knows the 1000–1 rule. A thousand hours of practice for every competitive star performance.

The idea of effortless superiority, of practice-less winning really is a movie myth. Sure, talented people pick up skills and knowledge faster and better, but it still takes effort. Wasted talent is untutored, untrained and unexplored talent. Getting into the talent group does not, or should not, in itself indicate anything more than you are judged to have something worth exploring. And if you don't or can't, you're out.

Next, is the issue of ability. Usually cognitive ability: the dreaded "i" word: intelligence. Companies still hesitate to assess their recruits with thorough cognitive testing. Usually, a minimum score will do. You need to be bright enough. Difficult to imagine organizational talent without brains. Ability endureth: easy to spot and measure from an early age.

Ability is important because it relates to the "pick up" speed and efficiency of knowledge and skills. As you go up within the organization, your tasks become more complex. You have to widen your skill set. You need more and more subtle soft skills: negotiation and persuasion, presentation and emotional intelligence. But you also need to learn new hard skills as technology changes, and to anticipate future patterns and trends. A touch of real, useful creativity might help.

The final part of the definition is the word "apply." It's about putting learning into practice. No point in acquiring knowledge and skills that one cannot or will not use. The whole point of business degrees is not to increase the promotability and income of the holders. It is to give salient knowledge and skills that will subsequently be applied in an organization. We all know the clearly talented peer at school or university whose career, rather than being stellar, stalled somewhat. Perhaps they are happy among the lower-middle ranking "also-rans." Perhaps we mistook them for having talent that wasn't really there. Perhaps they just did not have the stomach for the arduous journey.

61 Strong situations

People behave much the same in "strong situations," a lecture, a religious service, a military parade. Strong situations provide unambiguous clues about what is required. As a result, you don't observe many individual differences.

Consider most formal situations – the conference, the business dinner, the presentation to the board. There is an etiquette to these situations. Indeed, there are books that tell us how to behave. We learn good form: how to address an ambassador, how to choose and use cutlery at the table, what are, and what are not, acceptable topics of conversation.

The boot camp aims, like the parade ground, to iron out individuality. So do the prison and the monastery. In the old days, the psychiatric hospital did this. Uniforms, timetables and strict rules meant everything from your unique characteristics was removed. Hair was covered or shaved, body shape disguised and language limited.

It is the strong situations, not the personalities in them, that determine behavior. The most famous of all psychological studies have demonstrated that. The Milgram Obedience Study shocked people (pun intended) by demonstrating that paid volunteers of all sexes, ages and backgrounds would administer painful, even lethal, electric shocks to another person if told to do so by an authoritative experimental psychologist.

Acts of great heroism and self-sacrifice, as well as those of gratuitous evil, have been seen to be almost banal because they were so ordinary. That is the experience of those who met winners of great gallantry medals such as the Victoria Cross, and it was also true of those who met top Nazi or Khmer Rouge officials. They seemed so ordinary. But they did incredible things in usually strong situations.

There is a script for strong situations that most people follow. It tells us little of their individuality, their personal hopes and ambitions, values and skills, drives and passions. So, what has this got to do with business? Well, everything. Starting with the selection interview. To what extent is the traditional interview a strong situation that, by definition, reduces the show of individuality?

Interviews are very scripted, very predictable. There are endless self-help books that "ensure" you will be selected if you follow their 10-step plan. Then, there are books of "killer questions" that are bought by hopeless interviewers! Of course, there are also those on "killer answers" bought by insecure interviewees.

The interview is theatre. You have your costume and lines, there is a set – it's a test of presentation skills. What to wear? Formal, smart, fashionable but neat, clean and elegant? What if you wore multi-colored socks or lavish bling? Too risky? Breaking "the rules" even slightly can send strong messages. But are they received in the same way in which they were sent? Does the loud tie scream "attention-seeker" rather than be creative, do the pearls say dowdy and out-of-touch rather than chic? So, it's best to play safe and show little of one's real self. Indeed, some of us have "interview outfits" never worn except for those occasions.

Then there is the script. First, the "settle down" questions about travel to the interview, then some general ones about motives for the application, a few picking up information about the CV and, finally, one or two quirky questions. Then, of course, your turn to ask a question – it is after all an interview.

The well-prepared interviewee can usually anticipate most of the questions and, hence, prepare good answers. Answers that speak to their drive and their integrity, their capacity for hard work and their willingness to go the extra mile for their employer. The really clever ones go to the website of the company and do a little investigative homework to find the competency framework favored by the organization. This gives them the advantage of knowing the criteria by which they are being evaluated.

So, the wise prepare well for the interview. They know their lines and the plot; they wear the right costume with the right make-up, and they co-ordinate their verbal and non-verbal behavior perfectly to accentuate particular emotions.

Interviewers, on the other hand, have more latitude. But two things mean they do often follow a script pretty rigorously. *First*, some selection interviews are also seen as "selling opportunities." The interviewer sells the benefits, strengths and assets of the organization. They have glossy materials, dress up and choose favorite rooms to conduct interviews. *Second*, many believe it is professional to follow a pretty strict routine. They know the structured interview is best where all candidates are given the same questions in the same order for the same reason. All very predictable, very standard.

And so the method used to find out about individual candidates fails badly because it is a strong situation. A charade, a theatrical production where neither speaks honestly. That is why interviewers are interested in hobbies, pastimes where the "real you" manifests. What of the interviewee who admits to "bunjee jumping," "sky diving" and "go-cart racing," or one who admits to amateur dramatics, competitive contemporary dance or leading the girl guides?

The real person is seen when off guard: in weak situations. Perhaps you learn more about the interviewee, about how they behave in the waiting room before the interview and what they do after the interview than in it. Assessment centers are more valid because they last longer and consist of multiple exercises. And this is why universities now look at *Facebook* entries to find out what people are really like. It gives a somewhat different picture to the carefully submitted CV.

62 Superego vs. super ego

The Freudian word for conscience is *superego*. Sigmund's theory involved three characters: the selfish, primitive, gratification-demanding *id*; the reality-aware *ego*; and the still voice-of-conscience; the *superego*.

According to the theory, the conscience develops as a function of socialization and training. We are not born with it, but have the capacity to develop it. We progress on the rocky road from "polymorphous pervert" to responsible, rule-following, moral human being. Well, some of us do!

We wrestle, according to the Freudians, with those twin demons "sex and violence:" the essential ingredients of a great movie. We have to curb the *id*'s desire for immediate gratification on the sexual front, and resist the urge to beat up people who frustrate us. As social animals, we need to learn respect for others, empathy and selflessness rather than selfishness.

Psychologists have long been interested in moral development: how, why, and when children learn to be responsible, moral citizens. And why some get a bit stuck. Theologians, of course, preceded them, giving numerous pieces of advice on child-rearing so they know the still, quiet voice of conscience.

Business was late to discover the superego. Perhaps it is now manifest in all those courses on *business ethics*. Twenty years of scandalously greedy and immoral behavior by top business people made business schools examine their "moral training," or lack of it. So, the topic was invented and thrives.

Students often see business ethics as an easy option. Not like the challenging topic of finance or accounting. Further, the organizational behavior course has seen its share of superego sensitivity. So, the leadership lecturers talk of "servant leadership" (see Essay 56). And they have discovered this curious thing called "spiritual intelligence."

It appears, further, that a conscience is actually good for business. Kindness, empathy and compassion drive employee engagement, which has a direct impact on productivity and profit. That sort of thing. Not a great deal of evidence, but a nice idea.

But sitting alongside all this ethical morality and conscience talk we have the self-confidence, self-help literature. Young people have been told that self-belief is the only thing they need to fulfill their dreams. It is argued that self-confidence, not ability, drives performance. As a consequence, there has been an army of self-actualization trainers helping people to find their inner self – their real self and their real talents.

The positive psychology movement that, to some, suggests that you ignore your weaknesses (read "challenges") and work only on your strengths has helped this trend. So, too, has the *appreciative enquiry* chaps, who eschew criticism of all kinds.

Finally, the most widely used personality test in the world owes something of its popularity to the naïve, erroneous and misleading assumption that, whatever your profile, it is OK. And the profile of paedophiles, psychopathic murderers and liars?

These trends over the past few decades have seen the emergence of a cult of narcissism. Generation Y is characterized by its egocentrism, and a sense not of service but, rather, of entitlement. They are the "me-people," not the "we-people."

They have, in short, *super egos* – a super-sized sense of self, of their rights (not responsibilities), of what they are owed (not owe). "Ask not," said Kennedy 40 years ago, "what your country can do for you; ask what you can do for your country."

Those who supported all the "self-confidence predicts performance" literature did so with more belief than data. Sure, they are related – but whence the direction of causality? Successful people are self-confident as a result of their success. Teach people how (through hard work and practice) to be productive, and the rewards of that productivity will strongly enhance their sense of self-worth. Teach them only how to be more self-confident and you nurture arrogance, hubris and narcissism.

Selfishness is ego; selflessness, superego. The X factor perhaps illustrates most dramatically the problem with egotism. Frequently, talentless, plain (bordering on the unattractive) candidates, acting with childlike disbelieving rage when they are given self-evident feedback on their dismal performance. They get their just come-uppance for the first time, it seems, and they act with rage.

What happened to their sense of pride; dire warnings of hubris; a distaste for arrogance? Aren't our business leaders encouraged by PR to talk themselves up? The CEO with a big super ego is likely to have narcissistic, possibly anti-social, personality disorder. That super ego, easily suppresses the still, quiet, meek voice of the superego in business settings. Hence all that stuff about dodgy, immoral, superbly confident captains of industry.

So, the question is: Are the two related? Can one have a big superego and ego? Which one works best in business? Does the over-developed superego effectively inhibit people in that cut-and-thrust, dog-eats-dog jungle we call the marketplace? Or does it make for good leadership and good governance, and sustainability over time.

Certainly, the market likes a confident leader: so do the media and the staff. But an over-inflated sense of self is deeply unattractive. Humility is always more attractive than hubris.

Everyone needs a moral compass. Sure, we need to know where that thin line is between the spirit of the law and the letter of the law. And we need to appreciate the consequences of wrong-doing for self and others. Strong superego, moderate ego then.

63 Taking an HR exam

The University of Everyman has recently noticed the trend for middle-aged, under-qualified HR-people, scared of losing their jobs, to do a part-time degree in HR studies. This has been very popular and the course was over-subscribed. To get some idea of its contents, one can look at either the syllabus or the first exam paper.

The following is the three-hour, written, exam for the higher diploma:

Exam

WRITE SHORT NOTES ON 7 OF THE 21 QUESTIONS:

1. Clever behavioral geneticists have showed that job dissatisfaction is mainly heritable, and not due to nasty bosses or companies without HR processes. That is why some people go from one (damn) job to another, always being "pissed-off." What advice would you give to a (poor sodding) manager who has to deal with the genetically dissatisfied employee?
2. Should the head of HR change their title to *Chief People Person*? If not, come up with some equally vacuous, but pretentious, title.
3. It is wise to call in (sexy but very expensive) management consultants to justify, with clever stats, graphs and models, the reason why you have to down-size or right-size in the current climate because they can take the blame. Discuss.
4. "It is only really low moral fibre neurotics that experience stress at work." Draft a pretty cross letter to contradict this highly reasonable assumption.
5. Talent management is all the rage. How do you keep secret the fact that some pushy, spoilt, narcissistic young turks are not among "the chosen" and are effectively talent-less?
6. You can now do many post-graduate qualifications in training, organizational development or some other non-subject. Justify:
   (a) You not having one of these pointless pieces of paper.

(b) Why the one you have is essential to your job.

(c) Why "experience" (whatever that is) trumps all this credentialism nonsense.

7. Most executive coaches tend to be "let go" HR people with delusions of grandeur, little experience, but a taste for preposterous invoices. Draft a letter to this effect to some derailing middle-manager who thinks a coach might save him.

8. What happened to competencies? Have you updated your tired old list, or are you a constant fiddler? And how (really) unique is your list compared with practically everyone else's? Write a critical essay admitting that no one ever knew what they were, whether you could train them, or whether they were related to one another.

9. Working from home: a wise move to improve both productivity and satisfaction in long-commuting staff, or a modern excuse for staff effectively to take days off?

10. We used to call it "job satisfaction," then it became "commitment;" now it's called "engagement." Are you up to speed with this stuff, and can you get ahead of the game yourself by coming up with the next crazy term?

11. Doing climate/morale surveys is good impression management: it looks as if management really cares, wants to know, is eager to change. What do you do when the results come in, and it is apparent the whole organization is hacked off with practically everything, particularly your new grading system and long-standing appraisal system?

12. Work–life balance is really a girly issue: most senior chaps like to stay at work where they have support, seem to be taken seriously, and don't have to do child-care, shopping or chauffeuring. Discuss.

13. *Dress down Friday* is now old hat. Come up with some (equally daft, inane) cost-free idea that supposedly increases satisfaction, productivity and sociability.

14. When did you last tinker with the organizational chart (now called the "organogram")? What about the flat organization, stopping the *silo mentality* and clarifying the meaning of dotted lines all over the place. Rationalize all your own sins of omission and commission in this regard.

15. Only senior HR people know all the real details about how much people in the organization are really paid. How do you stop yourself from feeling furious about all the inequities that you see and whistle-blowing the local paper?

16. Senior managers won't go on your training courses because (they say) they are a complete waste of time, full of psychobabbly tosh and frequently humiliating. What sort of bribe can you use to whip them into line?

17. Health and safety is now a laughing stock with all their kill-joy pettiness, daft injunctions and litigious-phobic rule-making. How do you stop being tarred with the same brush?

18. Diversity at work: a marvelous chance to punish all those pompous, conceited, pale males; or the nightmare of finding enough minority people who can really do the job?

19. What HR books do you have on your shelf? Can you quote (anything) from Ulrich, who is everyone's number 1 guru? List a few books or authors whose books are "in" and those who are now passé.

20. Is bullying at work:
    (a) A serious problem that we have (mysteriously) overlooked for years.
    (b) An excuse for indolent neurotics to cause mayhem by laying charges.
    (c) Only ever done by low emotionally intelligent managers from engineering or IT.
    (d) The last resort of managers to get poorly-selected, lazy sods to do some work.

21. Which of the following courses are hardest, dullest and least important for HR managers? Rank order them:
    (a) An update on employment law.
    (b) HR from an EU perspective.
    (c) Financial management for non-financial managers.
    (d) Mastering HR IT systems.
    (e) New directions in health and safety.

64 Three journeys

There are only three kinds of jobs: technical, supervisory and strategic. Most people are selected on the basis of their technical knowledge and skills. These may be either relatively easy or difficult to acquire. They may require years of training, or be mastered in a matter of weeks. A brain surgeon and a fighter pilot, just as much as a tree surgeon and a bus driver, all have technical a job.

Technical jobs are evaluated primarily on skills and knowledge. These often take many years to acquire through learning, training and experience. They may be learned on the *apprenticeship* model, such as that of carpentry or academics, the *teaching* model or the *experiential* model. A newly-trained doctor or driver, accountant or actuary, cook or carpenter has acquired the expertise to do the job.

All managers want motivated staff. No matter how technically competent an individual, if they are not motivated to work hard they can be difficult, demanding and expensive. Hence, selection procedures are about what a candidate *can do* as much as what they are *prepared to do*.

Over time, if the recruit is good at the job, promotion may be offered. There are essentially two types of promotion. The *first* is to be made a senior "X" such as a senior train conductor, a senior house doctor, a senior lecturer. This means, usually, more money and more difficult tasks, or simply a reward for loyalty and confidence. Technical people are recognized for their ability and expertise and, through experience, are asked to do more complex, difficult and demanding tasks within the same area. Promotion is a reward for doing more challenging work.

Some technical people thrive at their tasks. Because of their aptitudes, temperament and values, they discover they are "the right peg in the right hole" and are able to exploit their talents. They do, every day, what they like doing most, are often extremely good at the tasks and, hence, highly effective, efficient and productive.

However, there is a *second*, very different type of promotion. This involves **supervision**. It means doing less of the task oneself, and monitoring and controlling others. Whilst supervisors often do a great deal of "the task" themselves, their newly promoted role is supervisory. In essence, others report to them, requiring help, guidance, and instruction.

It is the job of supervisors to get the best out of those who work with, and for them. They need the ability to plan, organize and control but, more than that, they need the ability to **engage** staff. Job satisfaction, commitment and engagement are, to a large extent, a function of a supervisor.

People move from supervisor to junior manager, even to senior manager, essentially doing the same job.

For many, the problem is "letting go." What supervisors have to let go is the temptation to do the job themselves. Often, this is a job they loved and were extremely good at, hence their promotion. Supervisory jobs are much less "hands on" and more "hearts on." It is about helping, about aspiring and supporting others to do the task. It is about coordinating and achieving goals *through others*. Hence the importance of interpersonal skills.

Promotion from a supervisory to interpersonal-management job is also recognition of effort and ability. The *third* type of job is *strategic planning*. This is usually thought of as a "board-level" job. At this stage, a person – often a senior manager, or possibly a general manager – to a large extent relinquishes the job of managing and supervising others. The task moves on to giving direction. Strategy is about the future. People at the strategic level have to learn to "read the signals" from the future. What is coming down the line? What are the opportunities or threats to the company? No organization can afford to stand still and become complacent. Global competition soon puts paid to organizations without insight, planning or strategy. "Third-level" top, strategic jobs are about the future.

There is often a large number of highly ambitious people who are eager to join the board. To do so, they have to master their supervisory jobs, but also show they are competent at strategic planning.

This involves looking more *outward* than inward. Strategists need to look to the future as well as the present, and they need to look around them at competition. Changes in technology, in customer expectations and in population, as well as regulation, can mean a successful organization can potentially go under overnight.

The strategist's job is to plot the journey to the future. It is partly an analytic and partly a planning function. But, perhaps more than anything else, it is a job that requires the selling of the leader's plan, mission, and vision. A brilliant strategy that no one understands or believes in is, essentially, a failed strategy.

Strategists need to align and motivate their staff, often through charismatic speeches and clear documents. They need to inspire the confidence of all their staff. They need integrity and, most of all, to be inspirational.

The problem is whether the skills, temperaments, values and preferences are very different in the three different jobs, and whether one can possibly be successful in them all. Often techies make terrible and unhappy managers. Sometimes, those with real strategic skills do not have their talents recognized.

65   Time at work

There will be fewer full-time and more part-time jobs – so we are reliably informed. There will be fewer core and more contingent workers. More people will work from home. Work will be a thing you do, not a place you go to. Certainly, the old 9-to-5, tea boy to managing director, pipe and slippers at 65 concept of work has gone.

Many new jobs carry various time options. Variable hours (flexitime, annualized hours, zero hours), restructured hours (compressed week), or reduced hours (part-time, job share or phased retirement). What are the options and what are the issues?

Part-time employment: defined as working less than 30 hours per week. These jobs can be very varied and categorized as permanent vs. casual, good vs. bad, voluntary vs. involuntary. More and more jobs fall into this category. More organizations are establishing policies, practices and procedures for part-timers; promoting part-time work as a legitimate alternative to full-time work and suitable for older workers. Cynical, cost-saving, or enlightened adaptiveness?

Contingent employment: defined as when an individual is working for an organization, but is not considered a regular employee. These include temporary, casual and technical contingent workers. This requires designing new ways of managing and motivating contingent workers, providing equitable treatment and protecting their interests.

Flexitime: defined as when employees vary their starting and quitting times, but are required to work a standard number of hours within a specific time period. This may have the staggered shifts concept, which is designed to discourage all workers arriving or leaving at the same time. This helps the work–life balance – which most people appear to like, and is seen as a stress reliever. Flexitime means establishing selection and eligibility criteria, and successful implementation procedures, and ensuring its compatibility with other organization initiatives.

Compressed working weeks: defined as re-allocating work time by condensing the total hours in the traditional five-day working week into fewer days. So, you could have a four day week, or a nine-day fortnight. This is popular, though its effects on productivity are unknown. Four challenges are specified:

- Identifying jobs that are appropriate for compressed working weeks.
- Identifying which compressed working week form is best.
- Preparing employees for compressed working weeks.
- Preparing managers and supervisors to manage these workers.

Tele-working: defined as working at a location away from the traditional place of work, full- or part-time, and involving the use of telecommunications and the electronic processing of information. Again, four challenges of this working type are identified:

- Ensuring a supportive environment.
- Identifying jobs that are appropriate for tele-working.
- Establishing selection procedures and eligibility criteria.
- Training both tele-managers and tele-workers.

This is sometimes called *home-working*.

Short-term contracts: defined as being in some sort of employment for a very specific, often short, not necessarily continuous period of time. So, the military may have short-term commissions, which mean you sign up for five to seven years. And some argue that we will now all be on short-term contracts, as we will have to apply for our jobs every so often. An employer's charter: a worker's nightmare.

Self-employment: defined as working for yourself, but this concept is being stretched for tax and other legal purposes. It is possible that you work in, and for, an organization (nearly all the time) but that it suits many people for you to be officially classified as self-employed. What is clear, however – and very interesting – is that once people take the jump and become self-employed, they almost never, ever, elect to work for someone else again.

Interim appointment: defined as occupying a role for a short and very specific period of time. This is similar to the short-term contract, but is usually at a higher level. People are often parachuted into a position to perform a particular task that might be time-capped.

Annualized hours: defined as total annual work hours (at, say, 35–40 hours per week, minus holidays and public holidays) worked at various times (two weeks on, two weeks off), as agreed by employer and employee. There are, of course, health and safety issues, as well exploitation and efficiency concerns, with this intense and variable way of working.

Zero-hours/on-call arrangements: defined as being in a work pool from which you may be called. But this has a "mutuality of obligation" arrangement: the employer is not obliged to find work, neither is the worker obliged to accept what is offered. The worker is on call for the problems of "lumpy demands." Ideal for some, a terrifying sense of insecurity for others.

Job sharing: defined as two or more people sharing a job with all its repercussions. This can be very difficult to manage, as it is not always clear who does what and how performance management should, or could, occur. It can lead to very happy job sharers (if they can choose a partner and the working conditions), but also to the polar opposite. Much depends on how the rewards are apportioned: equally or equitably.

All rather complicated, compared with the good old times. But then, work really has changed significantly, as have families and how we live our lives. For some, this has meant more choice and a better work–life balance; for others, it has just been an increase in misery.

66 Time perspectives

You are working in a team on a very important project. You are dependent on others delivering on time. Your career future depends on a successful outcome of the task.

You email a crucial team member to enquire as to the status of his progress. He replies "I will .... have it ready in two weeks."

Consider the following ten expressions that might go in the missing space:

definitely   hopefully   potentially   probably   possibly
likely   maybe   sort of   try to   unlikely

Consider each word and put a confidence percentage next to each. Thus, you may believe, if they say *definitely*, that you have a 90 percent expectation that it will be done, whilst *possibly* yields only a 30 percent expectation.

It is most fun to do this exercise in a multinational group, because wide variations occur. It shows how they encode and then decode rather differently. Just as in some cultures it is impossible to say "no," so, in others, probabilities are coded rather subtly. Thus, to say one cannot, or will not, do something sounds rude or like being insubordinate. So, the issue is coded somewhat differently.

The British do under-exaggeration (and self-deprecation); the Americans, over-exaggeration – but, with luck, they understand the codes of their people. However, the problems arise when dealing with those who are not co-nationals and coded messages are misunderstood.

But this issue is also about notions of time. All cross-cultural researchers are very aware of the fact that people think and talk about time differently. Some countries are *time-bound* (Germany, Britain, Switzerland, Scandinavia), whereas others are *time-blind* (Spain, Portugal, Greece). Time-bound societies emphasize schedules, deadlines, time waste, timekeeping, a fast pace of life. Time-blind societies are more relaxed and casual about time.

Hence, what is late in one society is not necessarily so in another. As societies become more time-bound, they have a more competitive attitude to time and so "fast" is better. Hence fast-living, fast-eating, fast-tempo, manic-type work behavior emphasizing "catching up" and not being "left behind." Time-bound societies see time as linear; the time-blind, cyclical. Time-bound societies centre work around clocks, schedules, delivery dates, agendas, deadlines. This can make for serious misunderstandings at work.

Then there is the time-blind culture's ability to distinguish between sacred and profane time. The former is for eating, family, sleeping. Profane time is used for everything else. Hence, in Spain, meetings can easily be interrupted; time is not dedicated solely to the meeting. There is also the distinction between *mono-* and *poly*-chronic time. Time-bound societies are monochronic – they do one thing at a time. The time-blind are poly-chronic, happily ignoring appointments, schedules, deadlines and tolerating interruptions.

There is also the issue of *time-orientation*: past, present and future. Thus, the British are thought to be interested more in the distant and recent past, and therefore do not invest so much in the future; the Germans have a longer view of the future, investing in basic research, education and training.

The understanding and use of time is crucial in business. Not only does it lead to how, when, where and why work is done but, also, people with conflicting ideas and theories may have very different conceptions and expectations. This can lead to miscommunication and animosity.

But, as with cultural differences, there are also individual differences. One distinction is between the *time estimator* and the *time contractor*. To the former, "I shall see you at 6.30" means any time around 6.30 (i.e. 6.05, 6.45); to the latter, that is a promise or a contract. If a time estimator is married to, or works with, a time contractor, all hell is frequently cut loose as their expectations and misunderstandings are challenged.

Equally, there are those fixated in the past, obsessed only with the present and those looking only to the future. Remembering past experiences and lessons is valuable. Concentrating on the "now" is important. Thinking about, and planning for, the future is good. But to be always backward-looking means you miss current opportunities, and to be so future-oriented that you ignore current problems impacts on how you get to the future.

Recently, Philip Zimbardo, in America, identified five key approaches to time perspective:

- **The "past-negative" type** – who focuses on negative personal experiences that still have the power to upset them, causing feelings of bitterness and regret.
- **The "past-positive" type** – who takes a nostalgic view of the past, with a "better safe than sorry" approach that may hold them back.
- **The "present-hedonistic" type** – who is dominated by pleasure-seeking impulses, and is reluctant to postpone feeling good for later gain.
- **The "present-fatalistic" type** – who doesn't enjoying the present but feels trapped in it, unable to change the future, feeling powerlessness.
- **The "future-focused" type** – who is ambitious, focused on goals, and a sense of urgency.

Our sense of time is shaped by personality and culture. Also, organizations have unique time cultures. Some do time-urgency seriously. Time is a measurable resource. Others seem much more relaxed. Some are amnesiac about the past, believing it pointless to look back. Others are obsessed with the future, paying top-dollar for strategy consultants to "predict" and, possibly, control the future.

67 Time-watching

Imagine a smallish city garden that was well-designed and planned by the previous owner of the house. It contains many beautiful flowering shrubs and has clearly been color coordinated. In the summer, it is colorful, beautifully scented and discrete: ideal for drinks parties.

But neither the owner nor their partner enjoys gardening much, though they do potter. Essentially, the garden needs two seriously good trims a year, with the removal of many bags of garden waste. So, over the years they have employed various gardeners.

It was the contrast between the two that was most enlightening about the issue of pay. Both did a good job and both received almost exactly the same remuneration. It was the time they took that was the difference, as well as their obvious success in life.

The first gardener was a plump and jolly woman. They later discovered she was on social security. She said she adored gardening and this garden (good marketing), and that she understood the brief. She charged by the hour, modestly.

She hummed and sang whilst at her task. She half-filled many sacks with clippings – a testament to her progress. She enjoyed a natter, as well as a bottle of beer around "close of play."

She took two-and-a-half days to do the job. The owners were rather pleased: the garden looked trim and well-shaped. She gave bits of advice about particular plants and appeared to leave happy.

The owners re-employed the hourly-waged gardener for a few more years, but then she went offline. So, they responded to a flyer offering the same service.

This time a male arrived with a truck. They showed him the garden which, being the same time of the year (eight months after the last gardener) was in much the same state. They described what they wanted: he gave an immediate quote, which was agreed, and he got started.

Six hours later he plodded through the house with fewer sacks of clippings, but these had been much more tightly-packed. The owners inspected his handiwork, approved and paid him. He tossed the sacks into his new-ish truck and left.

The piece rate worker had taken around 18 hours, he took around six. The output was similar: the work rate, style and philosophy radically different.

A one-off: quirky consequences of two idiosyncratic gardeners? Experiments require replications: the owners were to have evidence of this.

As well as the gardener, the couple also employs someone to do the ironing. They believe you should not do tasks you hate doing if you are able to earn money at tasks you like doing and can thus "trickle down" some money to those who do.

By chance, they had two home-helpers to do the ironing. Both Polish, both young, both careful. The regular person was paid by the hour for a range of domestic tasks including general cleaning, cooking, ironing and simple repair work. They noted how long she took to do certain things and tended to apportion her tasks by this calendar. Then the employers offered a job rate. These are the tasks; this is the money. Work at your pace by your standards.

The metric by comparison was number of shirts ironed. The "by the task" home helper ironed eight shirts, and undertook a wide range of simple and complex domestic tasks in three hours. The "by the hour" home-helper also did eight shirts in the same time. Was there a qualitative difference? No. Did they work differently: you bet.

So, what determines the different choices in charging? The gardeners could not have been different. One was an entrepreneur: captain of the ship, in a hurry; time was precious. They could make three times the money in the time earned by the hourly rate gardener and they knew it.

Is it personality, or value, or life–style, or aspiration that determines how self-employed people like to work? Is it perhaps determined by economic conditions?

68   The unethical manager

Management integrity is really important. Not just to please politically correct business ethics gurus, and not just because integrity is associated with theft and fraud – an increasingly common problem in (very) senior managers. Rather, it is because dishonest, low integrity, unethical managers lead to staff mistrust, which directly influences all staff attitudes and performance.

A bad apple rots the whole barrel. Unethical supervisors act as terrible role models. They corrupt the young, model dishonesty, cheat customers and reduce profits.

Having integrity is about knowing the difference between right and wrong, and putting that knowledge into practice. It is about good character and good conduct; fair play and honesty; following the rules (law) and justice. It is also about being consistent in what one says and does.

Most students of leadership recognize the central role of the integrity of leaders to their overall long-term effectiveness. People want trustworthy managers. Shareholders trust in the board. Followers do better with leaders who are less egocentric, selfish or unfair. So, why are people ethical or unethical; moral, immoral or amoral? Born or made? Situationally specific? Teachable? Too much else to worry about, or too academic a question? Perhaps. But what any professional wants to know is two things: how to select *in* the ethical manager and how to select *out* their "dark side" unethical brother; and how to design and maintain organization-wide integrity.

So, how to assess integrity? Whilst there are integrity tests, an obvious limitation of this method is that those without integrity lie. So, don't ask the individuals. Ask the people who *know*, such as their colleagues and their direct reports. And don't ask them about the person cheating, deceiving, stealing, and lying. Rather, ask about their lack of integrity: sins of omission rather than commission.

Consider the following statements used to evaluate your boss:

* My manager is always trusted by people in the workgroup.
* My manager always maintains high personal moral standards.
* My manager always tells the truth, even when it is difficult to do so.

- My manager always puts the organization's interests above his or her own.
- There is always consistency between what my manager says and what he/she does.

Note that the questions aren't about character (the manager is a bully or vindictive), or conduct (breaks rules, gets even), or personal issues (blames me for his/her mistakes). In essence, these ratings require people who know the manager to make estimates of the likelihood of him/her engaging in unethical behaviors. It asks people to rate the absence of integrity.

Imagine that once a year, as part of a 360-degree rating exercise, these and other similar questions were included in a test form that measured other aspects, such as the manager's vision, courage, energy and execution. Strictly speaking, a 360-degree (around the clock) appraisal means that, after individuals assess or rate themselves, they are rated by their bosses (top down), their peers (across), their subordinates (bottom up) and their "clients" (across).

The reasons for including their assessments are threefold. *First*, they have the actual data. They know. Through regular contacts, they have seen the manager behave under a wide variety of situations: when stressed or tempted or tired. They know typical, common and frequent responses to all situations, including those of temptation. *Second*, there are many of them, which means that if any one of them has a personal vendetta or grudge, they will show up as being different from the others. If they all agree the manager is of dubious integrity, beware. *Third*, they are much more likely to be honest than the managers themselves.

There certainly are problems. Raters need to believe you when you offer them anonymity and confidentiality. They also need to know you are going to take the results seriously and do something if they detect seriously unethical managers.

Whilst this approach measures the lack of integrity, it is important to understand what that means. Incompetence usually refers to the absence of some quality, whilst derailment implies the presence of something undesirable. A lack of integrity is usually accompanied by a lack of conscience: one sign of a psychopath.

Too many upbeat and simplistic management books have meant that the number of managers with "integrity issues" has been underestimated. This has occurred because traditional appraisal is conducted by the boss who rarely sees what subordinates routinely see – the "dark side," the dubious and duplicitous behavior.

The second big question is how to ensure the organization, as a whole, behaves with integrity. Putting integrity in the vision and mission statement is unlikely to do much. People expect integrity. Selecting in and out for integrity does help: look for signs and evidence of honesty and its opposite. Having increasing burdensome bureaucratic checks and balances often misfires.

Three things can and should be done. *First*, integrity has to be modeled from the top. Nearly two dozen American CEOs are in prison for fraud. They modeled corruption. *Second*, integrity issues need to be discussed, not pushed under the carpet. It needs to be pushed up the organizational agenda, not just a PR exercise to make people feel complacent. *Third*, everyone should know that integrity is assessed annually by and on all staff, and that the organization has a zero tolerance policy for unethical behavior.

69   Value clashes

A clash of cultures is often really a disagreement about values. It can be profoundly shocking to have to live and work with people who differ fundamentally in their values about little (tidiness) as well as big things (honesty).

Sometimes, the so-called "personality clash" at work is little more than a clash of values. So, what are values? Can they be assessed? Where do they come from? And why do people differ?

All societies, to some extent, value the same thing: family, tradition, honesty. They arise partly in an adaptive, evolutionary sense. Healthy, stable societies value trust and integrity, charity and humility. At the highest level, it is surprising how similar societies are, be they first- or third-world, hunter-gatherer or agricultural, Muslim or Christian, north or south.

We get our values from our society: primarily from parents, but also from schools, the media and our friends. The question is the power of each. A Jewish family living in a Christian culture, an ex-pat family living in a foreign culture, a neo-hippy post-materialist family living in an avowedly materialist society – all will strive to pass on their distinct values. The Amish religious values are a wonderful case study in how a small community can sustain a culture over time.

So, we acquire values. We don't inherit them genetically, though we do inherit both abilities and temperaments, which may influence the values we acquire. So, bright extroverts will value playfulness; conscientious people, order.

Values inform the way we see and make sense of the world. Most importantly, they influence our decisions. They filter and construct information. They are heuristic rules that often influence our decisions.

Values come in two categories. Terminal or "end state" values, which dictate life goals. To have or to be: equality vs. equity, innovation vs. traditional. They also dictate the method or "the how." These are instrumental values. So, it is not that difficult to define measures that profile a person's values. One can see whether they are interested in materialism or aesthetics; the extent to which they value charity over justice, humility over integrity.

One can describe these values at various levels from specific (i.e. neatness, orderliness) to the more general (conscientiousness, parsimony). Usually, but not always, they fit together. They make sense.

Surprisingly, perhaps, they are pretty stable over time. School reunions are often testament to this. People get wider, go balder and become wrinkly, but their values endure. Indeed, the values they had at school can often be seen to be the great drives in their career. Sometimes, they change radically. Trauma and therapy might do it. People can be suddenly, but very occasionally, converted to radical creeds. But you usually find they were the sort that was attracted to ideologies and -isms. To some outsiders, changing from orthodox X-ism to Y-ism is really not that dramatic a step.

But it is the last point that causes the biggest problem. People like those that share their values and, by corollary, dislike those that don't. Values bind groups. The criterion for entry and continual membership is the frequent public, verbal and behavioral endorsing of these values.

People choose groups and institutions like schools and jobs partly because of their values. Some would never join the police, work for an arms manufacturer or tobacco company, or even attend events sponsored by them.

And then the organization "socializes" one. This process is more obvious when witnessing cults, but it happens all the time. Hence the development of "group think," where people all think in the same way. They see problems and come up with solutions that are all similar to each other.

Soon values become internalized and natural. Value-driven beliefs and behaviors become normalized. Until, of course, you meet those who are "non–believers." The spender dates the saver; those fresh out of self-esteem therapy meet those who value humility; the Darwinian meets the Creationist.

A clash of values comes as a surprise and is a comparatively rare event, as we select our friends and work colleagues on the values that we share. It is easy for those who strongly value altruism to see others as deeply selfish; those who value tradition to be rigid authoritarians.

Because people are rarely confronted by others with very different values, they often find it difficult to defend their values coherently. So, they pick on other factors. Value clashes become personality clashes.

70   The valuelessness of knowledge

One university lecturer recently told her students their task was to "absorb the canon." By this, she meant they had to steep themselves in the acknowledged great works by extensive reading, re-reading and memorization. Those who absorbed the canon turned information into knowledge and thence wisdom.

Those who have "absorbed the canon" can quote it at will. It is the mark of a scholar: a person who, in conversation, would use a Latin or French tag or expression, would find the odd line from Shakespeare or the romantic poets succinctly and beautifully to summarize the point to be made.

All disciplines have a canon, but some rather more than others. Literature is the classic example and the arts in general, but the social and natural sciences also have their "classics." Perhaps the new departments or "merged" disciplines such as sports science or media studies are less canonical.

People are, or were, often in awe of those who had, indeed, absorbed the canon, because they know the ability and effort involved. Most religions believe, and strongly approve of, committing texts to heart. It is a sign of belief, of dedication and faith. The ability to recite by memory means you are literally a carrier of the truth. You don't need the text because you have absorbed it.

University courses still examine students' ability to memorize material. Wags have comically described university education as "where the notes of the lecturer become the notes of the student without passing through the minds of either and where, at a later date, a garbled version by the latter is *vomited up* to the former as proof of learning." Of course, the canon must be critiqued – or, rather, analyzed – in addition to being absorbed.

Psychologists have distinguished between two related but distinguishable types of intelligence: *fluid* and *crystalized*. The former is all about problem-solving and analytic thinking. It is the ability to do Sudoku at lightning speed, or solve a Rubik cube. It is about the efficiency of analysis; of mental operation. Those with fluid intelligence seek to solve logical problems more easily and quickly.

Crystallized intelligence, on the other hand, is accumulated knowledge. This can be measured by general knowledge or vocabulary. People with really high crystallized intelligence do well at pub quizzes, and do well on all the topics – science and geography, sport and fashion, pop culture and history. The person with high crystallized intelligence is thought of as well-read, well-educated and knowledgeable.

Bright, curious people learn fast and remember well. They are told something once and it is enough. They retain and build upon what they learn.

People who do teaching or training in the East will tell you that some groups have a very clear view of education, where the educator is the full vessel who pours knowledge into the empty vessel who is the learner. The more, and more valuable, the liquid (knowledge), and the more the learner absorbs and retains, the better the knowledge transfer.

Knowledge is deposited in (virtual and real) libraries. People who "swallow" the dictionary are articulate, eloquent and verbally dextrous. They have a greater store of words. Knowledge is captured in books, which is why the number of books a household contains is an excellent index of the social class of that house.

Bookshelves in most houses contain an eclectic and eccentric mix of books. Dictionaries and novels, anthologies of poems and quotations, guide books and atlases, A to Zs and biographies. Some are consulted often; others, very infrequently. They come in useful for homework exercises as well as wet weekends.

But how quickly are they becoming valueless and pointless? Who would struggle through the small print of a London A to Z when you can Google a beautiful, clear, multi-colored map with your individual route on it? Why bother with encyclopaedias at all? Once the greatest and most valuable repository of knowledge, they are now relics used mainly to decorate country hotel fake libraries. Libraries can be stored on a memory stick.

Information used to be obtained from people or books. Both were costly. Both involved investment. But no more. The verb "to google" means to have immediate access to all knowledge. Well, nearly all knowledge. There do remain secrets.

As the web grows, so libraries decline. Why visit them, students complain with some justification. All knowledge, at least information, is open to all. You don't need to have access to a great library to do scholarly work. Your home library is worthless – a dust-collecting, space-hogging, fire risk.

So, is all that effort involved in turning your brain into an information resource a waste of time? Why clutter up your head with stuff you can carry on a dongle or computer stick?

Some of the great universities have historically put less emphasis on the absorption of the canon than the critique of the canon. It is not how well you store information and knowledge, but how you critique and evaluate it. But this does not stop them having great libraries that are great repositories of knowledge. They know knowledge really is power … if wisely evaluated and applied.

71 What's the point of theory?

One criticism of many management training courses is that they are far too "theoretical." There appears to be, and often is, a serious gap between the expectations of the trainer and the trainee. It's worse if the trainer is a business school teacher and the trainee a high-powered, frenetic, no-nonsense, "practical" manager.

Trainees are, quite rightly, time-conscious. They attend courses to acquire skills and knowledge to improve their performance that (they hope) all have an impact on profit. That, at any rate, is the "return on investment" theory. Some are sent on courses as "punishment" because they aren't achieving; others as reward because they are doing so well.

A major problem with all courses is the issue of shared, agreed expectations of what they can deliver. What can you learn in a day, or even a week, at a training course? And what is the best way to learn? Listening or watching or doing?

Most of those who sponsor training – which can be fearsomely expensive – seem to target a mixture of attitudes, know-how and skills. They want the course to improve attitude (read "motivation"); they want the trainee to grasp new concepts for the changing business environment; they want a new skill set taught. All they are asking for is a totally committed, business savvy, emotionally intelligent graduate of a week-long course in a nice hotel.

From the trainers' perspective, the situation looks rather different. Trainers have the characteristics of those who go to the gym on New Year's Day. They want to lose 10 kg and be nicely toned, in a month. They certainly start off willing and eager but, as reality dawns upon them, things change. Fitness, like many things, involves a life-style change.

Trainers, teachers and business dons have a difficult job. The ones who do "fun and games" achieve good post-course, happy-sheet results, but there is usually very little evidence of any learning and everything is soon forgotten. The plodding, skills teacher can receive poor post-course evaluations but – with luck, and a bit of practice – some skills are retained.

But what of those who teach "the theory?" Theories such as behavioral economics, emotional intelligence, the theory of the firm. Worse, what if they teach different theories of the same issue: so, how about a lecture that compares and contrasts equity, expectancy-value and the latent needs theory of job motivation? Which one is correct, the naïve learner enquires?

What's the point of an academic-style lecture describing theories? After all, we know that an "academic question" is a semi-pointless one. We know, don't we, that academics rarely venture into the "real world." Isn't theory the opposite of practice? Amusing but irrelevant, and to be firmly locked up in the ivory tower.

Kurt Levine, a German-American psychologist, is famous for the saying "There is nothing as practical as good theory:" a typical academic, self-serving quote; or wise words?

Why is theory important? There are various answers. One is diagnosis and observation. People in business see trends. Sales, morale, absenteeism, defaults rise and fall. Why? Modern technology captures a great deal of data. But how to interpret it?

Good theories are explanatory, as well as descriptive. They may attempt to explain the relationship between two or more variables such as unemployment and inflation, or staff morale and shrinkage. Supply and demand is perhaps the best-known. Big theories "do" more variables and have more explanatory power. Big companies have in-house economists who are very theoretical chappies.

Theories help people make sense of observations because they describe and explain causal relationships. Theories that are consistently proven become facts. Theories help people see more; understand more effectively. Theories suggest hypotheses that can be tested.

Theories also suggest solutions to problems. If the cause is known, perhaps you can do something about the cure. The history of science is full of wonderful stories of how, serendipitously, people stumble upon things – such as the origin of diseases, or the properties of chemicals.

An elegant, succinct and parsimonious theory can be beautiful to behold. They are, perhaps, best in the workplace when they are counter-intuitive, such as theories to explain how monetary rewards reduce motivation, or where they offer better interpretation for observable events.

A good example of a helpful theory relates to the effectiveness of punishment vs. reward at work. Pilot trainees were observed to discover whether, when learning how to land aircraft, they improved more if given a vicious reprimand after a poor flight or a generous reward after a good one. The observers were clear: only punishment works because, after punishment, the pilots improved; after reward they only got worse.

However, the instructors were not aware of the regression to the mean theory in statistics, which explained the phenomenon quite differently. Very short parents often have children taller than them; very bright parents bear children of somewhat lesser gifts. All extremes become less so – very bad *and* very good. So, a very bad flight (subsequently punished) led to a better one, and a very good flight (subsequently rewarded) led to a less good one. The reward vs. punishment looked as if it was having an impact, but it was an illusion.

Of course, theories can be dangerous. Clinging onto an outmoded, disproven, inaccurate theory can be deadly in business. Theories are there to be tested. But some can be comforting and deeply misleading. People can be fundamentalist about theories, refusing to acknowledge their shortcomings.

Theories that explain everything – like communism or psychoanalysis – tend to be the most dangerous. They inspire dedicated, uncritical thinkers who pursue agendas with zealotry.

Theories have to be tested, refuted and critiqued. They are living things, particularly in business. But they are powerful tools to thinking and action.

72 Who wants to be an entrepreneur?

Being an entrepreneur is sexy. The *Dragons' Den* (a TV program where budding inventors and entrepreneurs present their idea live in front of four people who compete to question and back them) has turned half a dozen people into media stars. Governments, even of a pinkish hue, recognize the advantages of having wealth-creators in their midst. We have initiatives to encourage, nurture and promote entrepreneurship among the young.

But can you teach entrepreneurship? It is fashionable to believe that everything is "teachable." Take, for instance, creativity. There is a general, evidence-free and quite preposterous assumption that *everyone is creative*, and that all teachers need to do is somehow encourage it.

Thus, we have:

- The *arson school* – which helps you set fire to your creativity.
- The *constipation school* – which unblocks and enables you to express your innate creativity.
- The *liberation school* – which sets you free from the shackles that imprison you.
- The *discovery school* – which helps you find your inner creative being.
- The *Blue Peter School* – which enhances creativity through fun and games with toilet rolls and washing up liquid bottles.

Creativity, like all other human attributes, is normally distributed: a few extremely creative people and a roughly equal number, sadly, possessing little or none. Most lie in the middle of the continuum. Yes, you can teach creativity tricks and processes, but you won't achieve much without talent … or motivation.

The same is true of entrepreneurs, who clearly come in different categories. We have all witnessed the *avaricious* (*hopeful*) entrepreneur with a good idea that might make a fortune and apparently stimulates unquenchable greed. Then there is the *boffin inventor* entrepreneur with imagination, but no business savvy. There is, also, the *wide-boy* entrepreneur whose disrespect for the law and for proper procedures only takes him part of the way to his goal.

Certainly, entrepreneurs have to be strongly motivated. Most have early failures, but they get up, dust themselves down and ask what they learnt from the experience. They are innovators and risk-takers and early adopters. And they take the long view. Interesting how few had the goal *just to be rich*. Money is a metric not a goal. The more you chase the "elusive dollar," the less likely you are to grab it.

Of course, entrepreneurs come in different guises: the arbitrageur and the financier; the innovator and the contractor. And yes, they do seem to have some recognizable traits: persistent and persuasive; ambitious and able; self-confident and success-oriented.

Those who have studied successful entrepreneurs have tried to identify those characteristics that mark them out. Of course, studies differ and the results are "somewhat equivocal," but they show two things. *First*, that self-confidence, expertise and persuasiveness are not enough: necessary (in optimal amounts), but not sufficient.

Second, that there are three approaches or competencies that mark out the successful entrepreneur. They are *proactive not reactive*. They don't believe in having luck: they make it. They don't wait for opportunities, they create them. They have always, do always and will always show initiative: try something out, question whether things could be done differently, move against the norm. Together with this, they tend to be assertive: they stand up to be counted, put their heads above the parapet, are the tall poppy that is not afraid to stand out.

But perhaps it is their *achievement orientation* that most obviously marks them out. Committed, determined, decisive. Look into the history of those entrepreneurs who have started successful businesses, production units, new processes and you will soon see certain hallmarks. These include great concern with *efficiency* in all guises.

Things are systematically planned and executed. Monitoring systems are put in place. There is great concern for consistent, high-quality work. It is not about greatest profit or mark-up or returns. It is about getting it right, achieving the best, getting ahead of the crowd, being distinctive. This can mean looking out for, noticing and acting on opportunities ... but this is not mere opportunism.

Third, they show *commitment to others*. They know the importance of relationships and that management is a contact sport. They honor their word and are well-known for it. They recognize the importance of all business relationships. They know about team-building. They are known for their reliability ... and, yes, integrity.

But entrepreneurs seem still distrusted. The very concept is foreign, hence our having to borrow the word from the French. Parts of the media and the left-wing press seem to portray the entrepreneur as a tax-dodging, ducking-and-weaving, individual hell-bent on becoming a rich playboy. They do exist, of course, though mainly in mafia-type businesses.

The real entrepreneur puts business first: always above pleasure, often above health, sadly above family. They take (well-calculated) risks and are able to live with uncertainty. Their goal is to grow the business, achieve something of lasting value. And, yes, some do "cash out," lose the plot and descend into infantile narcissism. But many find a greater reward in using their wealth to help others, rather than indulging themselves.

The entrepreneur as cultural hero? Perhaps. But, like all heroes, often rather ordinary, unremarkable people. Most are not from privileged backgrounds, which may in part explain their drive and determination. Not to be "a success" or make a pile, but start a business and win the race.

73 Working abroad

It takes a lot of money to send an employee abroad: travel, accommodation, family resettlement costs. And an embarrassingly large number "don't work out." They don't function very well. Some "go troppo." Others have to be repatriated. A great adventure and a golden opportunity turn into a nightmare. Divorce, drink problems, depression … a pretty grim legacy from what was meant to be a wonderful, once-in-a-lifetime opportunity.

Many organizations are happy to employ "the natives" at a junior level, but want tried-and-tested people from head office to go and run the show. They know how the business works and understand the culture. Their job is a sort of cultural franchising, or corporate colonialism. We need "our man" in charge, who is happy to show the locals how it should be done.

The question, then, is whom to choose to go abroad? Is it to be seen as a punishment or a reward? Much depends on *where* you are sent, *for how long* and *to do what*. There are many dilemmas to be resolved. Should you send relatively young people who are fit and adaptable, and can probably pick up the "local lingo?" What if they have a young family? And what if the spouse is not so keen? So, why not send a silver-backed alpha male on a "last tour" to shake up the natives. But that could prove very costly … and perhaps there will be few volunteers.

The problem of working abroad is the issue of adaptation … to the working conditions, the language, the food, the climate and the local customs. The issue is usually called "culture shock." You can experience it even whilst on holiday.

Culture shock has recognizable symptoms:

- **Strain** due to the effort required to make the necessary psychological adaptations; of having to listen more carefully, watch more intently, react more slowly. It is about being more self-aware and having to learn a whole new behavioral repertoire.
- **A sense of loss** and feelings of deprivation in regard to friends, status, profession and possessions. Sometimes one's status goes up, but the loss of the familiar, the friendly ear, the people to shoot the breeze with can count for a great deal when one is tired and fed-up.

- Being **rejected by** and/or **rejecting** members of the new culture. It is unpleasant being an easily identified outsider, a target, a source of envy. Attributes are projected: wealth, (im)morality, values. Worse still, if you really despise and dislike the natives.
- **Confusion** in role, role expectations, values, feelings and self-identity. Indeed, "what know you of England who only England know." It can feel like being an adolescent again: exploring who you really are, and what you (let alone your company or your culture) stand for. What does it mean to be a man, a boss, a father? Too much existential angst for an adult.
- **Surprise, anxiety, even disgust** and **indignation** after becoming aware of cultural differences. To be confronted by people with different attitudes to everything from food to hygiene, truthfulness to stealing, can be profoundly disturbing.
- **Feelings of impotence** due to not being able to cope with the new environment. One may be deprived of a sense of humor as a result of the language difficulties. Dealing with all authorities – especially professionals, and even "servants" – becomes challenging.

It is all rather bad news. It means an emotional rollercoaster, feelings of total despair and powerlessness, and often illness.

Culture shock doesn't hit for a bit. There are well-known phases in the process. Initially, there is the **honeymoon stage**, where everything seems wonderful. The people, the plants, the food are exotic and enchanting. There is much to be admired in the locals who are so friendly and approachable. Then comes the **crisis phase**: suddenly things are not as clear as you thought, people are not honest with you, nothing works properly. You can't ever get cool and there is no news of home.

But, with luck, this can lead to **recovery and adaptation**. You pick up enough of the language, the etiquette, the worldview. You become sort of bi-cultural.

What does this all mean? It certainly helps predict **when** people are likely to require help and support. Not for a bit, but three to six months down the line. And it partly shows how they might react. They often react most strongly to different concepts of time, and straightforwardness. They talk of perfidious, two-faced, hypocritical, corrupt staff ... often meaning they have not really decoded the signals properly.

The question is **who** thrives best, **where** and under **what** conditions. Certainly, some countries are easier than others. Multinationals, the

Foreign Office and others often rank order countries on various dimensions such as corruption, infrastructure and climate. Some offer a "hardship" package if one has to live in a compound (ghetto) where at least some facilities are provided. Some places simply have, as Sir Dennis Thatcher wisely observed, "a buggeration factor."

And what about the individual? It helps if they speak the language or pick up languages well. It helps if they are clever, sociable and resilient. But, most of all, it helps if they have good social support. And this means a happy family. That is why selectors now interview the entire family when sending a senior person abroad.

74 The young CEO

Is it true that policemen and prime ministers are getting younger? Would you be troubled or delighted to find your accountant, dentist or lawyer was 29 years old? Or would you prefer them to be 49 or 59 … or would you not really care? How about an 82-year-old baby boomer who refused to give up work – happy with them as your eye surgeon or tax accountant? Feel uncomfortable if your 747 flight desk crew were pushing 70? Quite different from a 76-year-old barrister? Or headmaster?

Consider the case of the CEO (or CFO or COO of a big, powerful, important company). After considerable considerations and expense, you are down to two. They are very similar in educational qualifications, personality and values, but one is aged 35, and the other 63. Who do you want? A much easier decision would be if it were 45 and 55, which is more likely to be the case. Ten years in middle-age does not seem that much, but a CEO in his thirties? Of course they exist, particularly in the high-tech industries.

The dynamics, the energy, the enthusiasm of youth? The understanding, the wisdom, the maturity of age? But it is the E-word that comes to mind. That vague and woolly concept called *experience*. Age says "seen it all before," "tried and tested," "a trifle premature." Youth says "do keep up," "move with the times," "try something different." Presuming they have the same formal training, older people (usually) have had the benefits of being confronted with, and hopefully solving, a wider variety of problems. They have something called "life experience:" being battered by the strong winds of difficulty and disappointment. Hopefully, this has made them rather than broken them. Life experience is the teacher. Managing, enduring, overcoming the unexpected.

But can experience imprison people as much as empower them? How often does one see people repeat, again and again, old formalities that once worked and that are no longer appropriate? To some extent, we are captives of our time. This is often seen in popular (as opposed to classical) music tastes. Many people are loyal fans of the music of their youth; sometimes the dress and the dancing, too. They can also be enchanted, encapsulated and even imprisoned by the technology of their youth. Hence, all those semi-pathetic middle-aged men playing with train sets.

What changes with age: many things of course, particularly in late middle-age, around 60. Physical health declines, though psychological health may not. But it is energy, speed and stamina that is most noticeable. We just slow down: physically, cognitively and, perhaps, emotionally. Given equivalence in ability and motivation, it is abundantly clear that young people learn faster.

So, back to the problem: the 35-year-old or the 63-year-old? What if you choose both, but have one deputy to the other? Which way around would work best? Neither seems very natural. The answer probably lies, *first and foremost*, in what sector the business is in. There are, perhaps, two things that are important: high-tech or manufacturing, pharmaceuticals or banking, transportation or government service. One central consideration is how fast is change in the sector? Is it a young person's business? So often the pharmaceutical industry is. Young people are more adaptive, curious, open to change. The managing of people is much the same everywhere, but the actual business/product and processes may be very different. The more change, development and progress in the area, the younger the CEO.

Second, there are issues of fitness and health. The stresses put on CEOs are immense. We are all bio-psychosocial animals. Our health is a function of our biology. Some people deteriorate faster than others. We all slow down and become more forgetful. That can be certainly very relevant to the carrying out of certain tasks.

References

Argyle, M. and McHendry, R. (1971) "Do Spectacles Really Affect Judgements of Intelligence?," *British Journal of Social and Clinical Psychology*, 10, 27–9.

Barbuto, J.E. and Wheeler, D.W. (2006) "Scale Development and Construct Clarification of Servant Leadership," *Group and Organization Management*, 31(3), 300–26.

Csikszentmihalyi, M. (1990) *Flow: The Psychology of Optimal Experience*. New York: Harper & Row.

Easterlin, R. (1973) "Does Money Buy Happiness?," *Public Interest*, 30, 3–10.

Fischer, C. (2008) "What Wealth–Happiness Paradox? A Short Note on the American Case," *Journal of Happiness Studies*, 9(2): 219.

Greenleaf, R.K. (1970) *The Servant as Leader*. Robert K. Greenleaf Center.

Herrnstein, R.J. and Murray, C. (1994) *The Bell Curve: Intelligence and Class Structure in American Life*. New York: Simon & Schuster.

Hudson, L. (1967) *Contrary Imaginations: A Psychological Study of the English Schoolboy*. Harmondsworth: Pelican.

Kets de Vries, M.F.R. (2006) *The Leader on the Couch*. Chichester: Wiley.

Pausch, R.F. (2007) "The Last Lecture: Really Achieving Your Childhood Dreams," September 18, Carnegie Mellon University. Available at http://www.youtube.com/watch?v=ji5_MqicxSo.

Snow, C.P. (1959) Rede Lecture, "The Two Cultures," 7 May, Senate House, Cambridge.

Swami, V., Chamorro-Premuzic, T. and Furnham, A. (2010) "Unanswered Questions: A Preliminary Investigation of Personality and Individual Difference Predictors of 9/11 Conspiracist Beliefs," *Applied Cognitive Psychology*, 24, 749–61.